Limited Government:
A Positive Agenda

JOHN GRAY
Fellow and Tutor in Politics,
Jesus College, Oxford

J. Frank Harrison

January 1990.

IEA
Published by
THE INSTITUTE OF ECONOMIC AFFAIRS
1989

First published in June 1989

by

THE INSTITUTE OF ECONOMIC AFFAIRS
2 Lord North Street, Westminster,
London SW1P 3LB

© THE INSTITUTE OF ECONOMIC AFFAIRS 1989

Hobart Paper 113

ISSN 0073-2818
ISBN 0-255 36221-8

Printed in Great Britain by
GORON PRO-PRINT CO LTD
6 Marlborough Road, Churchill Industrial Estate, Lancing, W. Sussex
Text set in Berthold Baskerville

CONTENTS

[3]

FOREWORD

The boundary between the market and the state is easy to sketch but virtually impossible to set down in detail if one does not adopt the extreme positions of anarchism, *laissez-faire* or totalitarianism. What does a limited government look like? What are its legitimate functions? What modes of activity and intervention should it use? These are questions about which people of the same philosophical disposition quickly disagree. The problem is more often than not resolved by ignoring it. This is particularly the case with economists. After developing grand theories about the operation of the economy, their policy prescriptions about the state are *ad hoc* and not often anchored in any practical agenda.

Most economists would say that the state should intervene to remedy the failures of the market-place and to bring about a more desirable (perhaps a more 'just') distribution of income. Others would pursue a more interventionist programme either by defining market failure in a way that rationalises interventions drawn from outside economics or by denying that market failure is the sole justification for government intervention. The public choice school interprets the boundary between the state and the market as the outcome of a private contest for wealth redistribution not to the poor but to the politically active and effective, played out in a political arena where government is the monopoly supplier of legitimate coercion.

The question of what the state should do and how it should do it is one that has challenged political philosophers and politicians for centuries. It lies at the heart of the society we want to live in and the economic and personal relations of its people. It is for this reason that the IEA has sought to encourage the debate on these fundamental issues by asking Dr John Gray to consider the question of the rôle of government from the point of view of the political philosophy of liberalism. The result is a thought-provoking analysis and discussion which is pregnant with ideas for further debate and controversy. Dr Gray's case for limited government and a market economy is not at root economic but ethical. It is that market institutions are the only ones that in practice permit individual autonomy and liberty.

[7]

Yet, as the reader will quickly find, Dr Gray is not an advocate of *laissez-faire* or constitutional limitations on government. Rather he sees a positive rôle for government—'a limited state with positive responsibilities'. It must develop and enforce a legal framework compatible with individual enterprise and liberty. Thus Dr Gray is a strong advocate of private property and private money. He proposes that the state should redistribute income to the poor and reinforce important cultural values. The last two rôles will meet with reasoned disagreement from other liberals and those who sympathise with Dr Gray's basic approach.

This *Hobart Paper* represents the views of its author and not those of the IEA. As an educational charity the IEA has as one of its principal objectives to publish scholarly works designed to educate and inform. Dr Gray's *Hobart Paper* achieves this aim by considering one of the pressing questions of contemporary society. The boundary between the state and the individual is hard to define in detail and subject to much popular misconception. Dr Gray, by putting forth his case will, we are confident, provide a new and important focus for the continuing controversy on the legitimate boundaries of the state in a free society.

May 1989   CENTO VELJANOVSKI

THE AUTHOR

JOHN GRAY was born in 1948 and educated at Exeter College, Oxford, where he received his BA, MA and DPhil. degrees. Between 1973 and 1976 he was a Lecturer in Government at the University of Essex. Since 1976 he has been a Fellow of Jesus College, Oxford.

Dr Gray's principal interests are in political philosophy and political economy. His books include *Mill on Liberty: A Defence* (Routledge & Kegan Paul, 1983); *Hayek on Liberty* (Basil Blackwell, 1984; Second Edition, 1986); *Conceptions of Liberty in Political Philosophy*, edited, with Z. A. Pelczynski (Athlone Press, 1984); *Liberalism* (Open University Press, 1986); *Liberalisms: Essays in Political Philosophy* (Routledge & Kegan Paul, 1989).

Dr Gray has contributed to the series of IEA Discussion Videos entitled *The World of Economics*, launched in 1987, on the subject of 'New Classical Liberalism: Challenges and Conflicts' (Guild Sound and Vision, Peterborough, 1988).

ACKNOWLEDGEMENTS

The task I was commissioned to undertake by Graham Mather and Cento Veljanovski, that of specifying the positive responsibilities of a limited government, has an hubristic aspect to it, since it involves commenting on a very wide span of policies. I have tried to discharge the brief I was given by focussing on areas of policy where I have some special interest or competence, and by seeking expert advice and criticism on many other issues. Aside from its specific policy proposals, the resultant monograph has a single, simple underlying theme. This is that the market economy is not a self-sustaining order, but depends crucially on an undergirding culture of liberty. This culture, in turn, cannot be protected or reproduced primarily by legal or constitutional devices; its vitality presupposes a good distribution of resources and opportunities, such that no significant sections of society are excluded from being beneficiaries of, and participants in, the market economy.

Policy over the last decade has in important respects freed up markets from the stranglehold of interventionism, but it has as yet failed to address itself to the cultural and distributional preconditions of a stable market order. Worse, policy in recent years has had a centralist momentum which has had the effect of weakening the autonomous institutions of civil society. In criticising this trend, and in assessing critically certain standard positions in neo-liberal theory and policy, my hope has been to break fresh ground, so as to open up new perspectives in the next phase of discussion and debate. Nor have I been deterred by the supposed 'political impossibility' of some of my proposals, since one of the lessons of the past decade in Britain is that today's political impossibility is tomorrow's conventional wisdom.

The influences of a range of conservative and liberal writers—Isaiah Berlin, Samuel Brittan, James Buchanan, F. A. Hayek, J. S. Mill, James Meade, Michael Oakeshott and others—will be readily apparent in these pages. A précis of this monograph was presented at the inaugural meeting of the Market Philosophy Study Group at the Institute of Economic Affairs. For their

[10]

comments at that meeting, I am grateful to Antony Flew, Shirley Letwin and Kenneth Minogue. For their very detailed and helpful written comments and criticisms, I am indebted to Barry Bracewell-Milnes and Tim Congdon. Andrew Adonis, Andrew Melnyk and Simon Upton are also to be thanked for their detailed criticisms. John Wood and David Green of the IEA made very pertinent and constructive observations to which I have tried to respond. My friend Norman Barry, while dissenting sharply from much in the theoretical portions of the monograph, gave me penetrating comments on several aspects of my enterprise. My colleague at Jesus College, Donald Hay, gave me incisive criticisms of many portions of my argument. Finally, I wish to thank especially David Willetts of the Centre for Policy Studies, whose comments on both the theoretical and the policy sections have proved literally invaluable to me.

Given the assistance I have had in this venture, it is particularly important to stress that I have sometimes stuck to my guns and rejected the advice I have been given. None of those whose help I have acknowledged is therefore in any way responsible for any of the arguments, conclusions or proposals advanced here. This is also true of Graham Mather and Cento Veljanovski, without whose support and encouragement the monograph would not have been begun, still less completed.

Much of the research undertaken for this book was done when the author was resident as Distinguished Research Fellow at the Social Philosophy and Policy Center, Bowling Green State University, Ohio. I am indebted to the Directors and staff of the Center for providing me with ideal conditions for thinking and writing.

May 1989   J.G.

I. INTRODUCTION:
THE NECESSITY OF CONSTRAINED GOVERNMENT

'. . . none of the precious "freedoms" which our generation has
inherited can be extended, or even maintained, apart from an
essential freedom of enterprise—apart from a genuine "division of
labour" between competitive and political controls'.

*primary
variable
is property*

HENRY SIMON[1]

The proper extent of the activity and authority of government is
the chief question in political philosophy. But the object of these
reflections is not to try to specify, once for all, the appropriate
functions of government and the limits of its authority. There are
good sceptical reasons—which I shall invoke when I consider
recent attempts to fix the frontiers of the state by reference to a
set of abstract principles—for supposing that that object cannot
be achieved. My purpose here is the humbler one of addressing
the role of government in Britain today. Since I deploy
arguments and considerations which ought to be accepted by
anyone who cares for individual liberty, my reflections may turn
out to have application well beyond our present circumstances
in Britain, but I harbour no aspiration of universality for them.
This is intended to be a study in theory and policy, not primarily
in political philosophy.

*1,
but ?
2.*

I shall not rehearse my arguments here, but instead simply
summarise my conclusions. The scope of government activity in
Britain remains vastly over-extended. The autonomous institutions of civil society are today threatened by an invasive state
whose size and arbitrary power have not substantially diminished, and in important respects have indeed been enhanced,
after a decade of rule by a Conservative administration
avowedly dedicated to whittling down government to its most
indispensable functions. In recent years, the project of confining
government to the task of assuring individuals and enterprises a
stable legal and monetary framework within which they may
plan their own activities has been abandoned, and there has

[1] Henry C. Simon, *Economic Policy for a Free Society*, Chicago: University of Chicago Press,
1948, pp. 41-42.

been a return to 'stop-go' policies of macro-economic management, with government conceiving of itself as the leader, sponsor or author of enterprise. According to most measures, the overall burden of taxation has not diminished but increased, and public expenditure as a function of national income has fallen only slightly.

Increasing Dependency and Centralisation

It is, again, a depressing fact that, despite efforts to diminish the culture of dependency in Britain, the poorer half of the population still receives nearly half of its income from government. Most ominously, perhaps, a tendency to increasing centralisation has become evident in many aspects of policy, particularly in those concerning education, with substantial discretionary powers being appropriated by Ministers. As *The Economist* noted recently:

'Far from reducing the role of the central state, Mrs Margaret Thatcher's government has extended it. ... Mr Kenneth Baker acquired 415 new powers when the Education Reform Act became law in July. ... Mrs Thatcher's government has also broken all records in the *quantity of legislation*.'[1]

There has also been an explosion of *secondary legislation*, with the first half of 1987 seeing as many pages of statutory instruments (allowing for subsequent ministerial orders) as the whole of 1959. Further, as *The Economist* went on:

'Over the past two years the civil service has started to grow again. Its numbers are still higher than they were under Mr Edward Heath's Tory government of the early 1970s ... The numbers working for quangos have also started to rise. Recent and pro-spective legislation could make things worse. The new education bill has created four big new quangos, covering the national curriculum, school examinations and the financing of universities and poly-technics. The water-privatisation bill will set up an even bigger one, a national rivers authority employing up to 10,000 staff.'

The danger we now face is that in the ruins of a project of limited government a corporatist monolith is being built up, which in the inevitable effluxion of time will be inherited by an administration (of any party) that, by conviction or by force of circumstance, will regard the claims of individual liberty with indifference or hostility.

[1] *The Economist*, 20 August 1988, p. 52.

The Limiting of Government – Role of Umpire

One of my two main claims in this *Hobart Paper* is that the project of limiting government in Britain stands in urgent need of reassertion. Measures must be conceived and implemented which halt and reverse the trend to centralisation, and return power and initiative to civil society. Reviving the project of *as what?* limited government involves adopting policies which effect a withdrawal of the state from many areas of social life and subject its remaining interventions to radical amendment. It means reaffirming the conception of government, most profoundly theorised by Thomas Hobbes and eloquently defended in our own time by Michael Oakeshott,[1] as first and foremost the protector of the peace and guardian of civil society. This is the first of my claims—that government in Britain must relinquish a paternal role in the economy and society, substantially withdraw from the sphere of civil life, and assume again its true office, which

> 'is not to impose other beliefs and activities upon its subjects, not to tutor or to educate them, not to make them better or happier in another way, not to direct them, to galvanize them into action, to lead them or to co-ordinate their activities so that no occasion for conflict shall occur. ...'; *to promote non-participatory lower orders*

the office of government is that of

> *whose rules?*
> 'the umpire whose business is to administer the rules of the game, or the chairman who governs the debate according to known rules but does not himself participate in it'.[2]

This is an understanding of government conspicuous by its absence in recent years from political discourse in Britain. *?*

The Positive Tasks of a Limited Government

My second, and perhaps more contestable, claim is that a government which is limited has nevertheless an important positive agenda to fulfil. This is to say that, whereas government is presently vastly inflated in its activities, what is needed is not a minimum state, but a limited or framework government with significant positive responsibilities. Let me mention the most weighty of these positive tasks. Government has a duty to *But!*

[1] For Oakeshott's interpretation of Hobbes, see Michael Oakeshott, *Hobbes on Civil Association*, Oxford: Basil Blackwell, 1975.

[2] Michael Oakeshott, *Rationalism in Politics*, London: Methuen, 1962, pp. 186-87.

emancipate the poor and the underclass from the culture of dependency and thereby enable them to act as full participants in civil society. It has an obligation to protect and promote independence and freedom of choice, by enabling all who wish to do so to acquire a decent modicum of wealth and to exercise responsibility in the control of their health, education and provision for old age. And it is a responsibility of government to facilitate the transmission of valuable cultural traditions across the generations. In this regard, it behoves government to acknowledge the diversity of cultural traditions existing among us in Britain by providing each with the opportunities and, where necessary, the resources whereby it can express and reproduce itself in peaceful co-existence with its neighbours.

These three tasks are not intended to be exhaustive of the positive functions of government in Britain today, but they seem to me to mark the chief areas where a limited government may and should go beyond its most essential rôle as umpire and peace-keeper. Discharging these tasks will require the abandonment by government of policies which have imposed on civil society the heavy burdens of chronic inflation and excessive taxation. Government can best discharge its positive duties, not by adding further to the ramshackle apparatus of the so-called Welfare State, but rather by dismantling it progressively and returning its resources substantially to the domain of private provision. A limited government will always have positive duties in respect of encouraging the relief of poverty and the diffusion of wealth, the support of education and health services and the protection of valued cultural traditions.

Moreover, a limited government has reason to concern itself with the distributive implications of its systems of taxation and welfare. In general, I will contend that, even though many of the central policies and institutions of the interventionist state require abolition rather than the sort of replacement for them that is envisaged in schemes for universal vouchers or negative income taxes, for example, there remains a range of positive services which government is entitled and obliged to provide as means to the ends of greater independence, freedom of choice and diversity in communal life. A limited government does most to achieve these ends, however, when it acts to repair and renew the fabric of civil society—the institutions of private property and contractual exchange on which a market economy, and thereby all the autonomous institutions of a free people, ultimately depend.

[16]

specious argument! BS.

presumed causal linkage

terms "progressive" ed "return" used in a highly rhetorical, non-empirical, conceptually imprecise manner

The Argument for Liberty and the Task of Philosophy

Many who have sought to defend individual liberty in our times
have supposed that its survival depends upon our having at our
disposal the resources of a comprehensive doctrine, a systematic
philosophy, on which our commitment to freedom is to be
founded, and from which the principles specifying the limits of
state intervention may be deduced. Bentham and J. S. Mill,[1]
each of them classical liberals by the standards of the revisionist
liberalism of later times, thought that the importance of
individual liberty in both its personal and its economic aspects
could be demonstrated as a derivation of the Principle of Utility.
Locke, Kant and, in recent years, thinkers such as John Rawls
and James Buchanan[2] have developed a far more persuasive
argument that the essential institutions of a liberal society can be
given a rational reconstruction as the outcome of an hypothetical
choice under conditions of uncertainty. Each of these per-
spectives has something to enrich the argument for liberty.

Utilitarianism—at least in some of J. S. Mill's writings, and in
later writers such as Henry Sidgwick,[3] before it was appropriated
by the theorists of welfare economics—comprehends the insight
that voluntary exchange in a market economy is the best guarantor of general welfare. Contractarian theory, especially in the
form in which it has been developed by James Buchanan, shows
why and how it is that a reconstitution of limited government
may be in the interests of each, and thereby of all. A third strand
of argument, that which invokes fundamental rights as the foundation of limited government, has less to offer the argument for
liberty, but serves as a useful reminder that the principal defence
of liberty is not in its promotion of efficiency or productivity, but
in its contribution to the liberty of the individual.

Each of these schools of liberal philosophy has something to
offer the argument for liberty, even though none succeeds in
giving individual liberty a demonstrative foundation in unshakeable first principles,[4] or is capable of serving as any very

---

[1] For an account of the utilitarian argument for individual liberty as developed by J. S.
Mill from the classical utilitarianism of Jeremy Bentham and James Mill, see my *Mill on
Liberty: A Defence*, London: Routledge and Kegan Paul, 1983.

[2] For an account of the contractarian argument for liberty, see my forthcoming *Liberalisms*,
London: Routledge, 1989, Ch. 10.

[3] For Sidgwick's account of 'the individualist minimum' of government, see H. Sidgwick,
The Elements of Politics, London: Macmillan, 1891.

[4] I argue this point more systematically in 'After Liberalism', Postscript to my book,
Liberalisms, op. cit.

definite guide to practice. As I see it, the value of political philosophy is prophylactic, in that it discourages us from expecting too much of general principles, and teaches us that policy and practice are always under-determined by them. The liberal perspectives I have mentioned—utilitarian, contractarian and rights-based—are illuminating and helpful as a compound of theory and rhetoric, rather than as exercises in philosophical inquiry. My approach will not be that of the liberal ideologue who seeks to give liberal values an unquestionable claim on reason, but instead that of a theorist of our own political experience and tradition. I will hold that its most essential elements, as well as its current vicissitudes and disorders, are best expressed in the thought of Thomas Hobbes, which (shorn of its contractarian metaphor and of its over-simple psychology) best conceives of government as the guardian of the peace that is attained in civil association. My approach will venture the paradox—a genuine paradox, in that it expresses a truth in the form of an apparent contradiction—that it is in such an Hobbesian conception, in which the state is unconstrained by antecedent rights in its pursuit of civil peace, that the best guide to an understanding of the character of limited government in Britain today is to be had.

On the theoretical side, accordingly, my task will be to elicit from our political experience a range of considerations which assist us in grasping the character of a civil society and defining the role of government in sustaining and reproducing civil society. Among such considerations are a concern for the autonomy and independence of the individual, the protection of these values by a rule of law, and the contribution made to individual liberty by freedom of enterprise in a market economy. These considerations, in turn, suggest on the policy side a series of maxims, intended to guide reform of the currently massively over-extended activity of government in Britain today, which in turn dictate a variety of broad policies to these ends. These maxims are not the 'unshakeable first principles' of liberal doctrine, since they are not intended to be universal in application, they are not derivable from any general theory of human nature or of historical development, and it is not supposed that they necessarily cohere into a system which obviates the need for trade-offs among conflicting values and interests. Such maxims are altogether humbler devices, aiming only to illuminate political experience in our tradition, and to

[18]

suggest profitable directions in the reform of our inheritance of civil society. The defence of these maxims is ultimately in terms of their contribution to human well-being, but it is the well-being of human beings, not in the abstract, but as we know them—the concrete, historically specific human beings who inherit the liberal tradition of individuality.

II. THEORY

'Freedom, like a recipe for game pie, is not a bright idea; it is not a "human right" to be deduced from some speculative concept of human nature. The freedom which we enjoy is nothing more than arrangements, procedures of a certain kind. . . . And the freedom which we wish to enjoy is not an "ideal" which we premeditate independently of our political experience, it is what is already intimated in that experience.'

MICHAEL OAKESHOTT[1]

The Fallacy of the Minimum State and the Mirage of *Laissez-Faire*

The scope and limits of government cannot be determined *a priori*. Time, place and historical circumstance are of crucial importance in determining the range and character of intervention by the state in civil society. To assert this necessary indeterminacy in the functions of government is to go against a powerful tradition in classical liberal thought, which has sought to specify the proper activities of government by a universal doctrine. The simplest (and least compelling) of these is the doctrine of the minimum state, which asserts that the sphere of government action is exhausted by the protection of negative rights. This is the doctrine espoused by von Humboldt, by Herbert Spencer and, in our own day, by Robert Nozick.[2] It has many difficulties, some of them fatal to it.

Most fundamentally, there is the difficulty generated by the vagueness of those negative rights which it is claimed the state has the duty to protect. Is there only one such right—to liberty, say—and, if so, how is it to be defined? (How are conflicts between one man's liberty and another's—between a sphere of privacy and the liberty of expression or information, for example—to be adjudicated?) If there are many such rights, how is practical competition among them to be resolved? The history of judicial review in the United States, which is founded on the

---

[1] Oakeshott (1962), *op. cit.*, p. 120.

[2] I consider the limitations of a rights-based doctrine of the minimum state, more systematically and extensively, in my *Liberalisms*, *op. cit.*, Ch. 9.

supposition that such rights exist and have a definite and ascertainable content, is a history of endemic and intractable conflict about them. In truth, because their content is open-ended and their very definition uncertain, the negative rights in terms of which the minimum state is theorised confer upon it all the indeterminacy which characterises my own account of the proper functions of government. That this is indeed so is only confirmed by the many contemporary theories of government which restrict its duties to rights protection, but affirm that there are positive as well as negative rights—rights to well-being or the satisfaction of basic needs, for example.[1] Such theories are not (as contemporary classical liberals insist) distortions or perversions of an earlier and legitimate theory of negative rights, but rather inevitable developments of a discourse of rights whose contents are incorrigibly indeterminate.

Classical liberal conceptions of the role of the state that are spelt out in terms of a principle of *laissez-faire* suffer from the disability that that principle is itself practically vacuous. In civil society, the sphere of independence is constituted by a most complex structure of legal immunities, forms of property, and personal and economic liberties—a structure whose specification is given us by no general theory. The contours of the sphere of independence are not natural truths, but instead artefacts of law and convention, subject to the need for recurrent redefinition and sometimes expressing a balance between competing interests and values. The ideal of *laissez-faire* is only a mirage, since it distracts us from the task of assessing our historical inheritance of laws and procedures and reforming it so as to promote the diffusion of power and initiative and thus to enhance the liberty and dignity of individuals.

The Idea of the Minimum State: An Empty Theory

Theories of the minimum state, then, are worse than uninformative—they are virtually empty of content. Even if we grant them a rough-and-ready sense, they are unrealisable. Government in Britain has never, even at its smallest, been the minimum state of classical liberal doctrine. We may regard the severely limited government that prevailed in the late 18th and early 19th centuries in England as embodying in many respects an ideal worthy of restoration. Nevertheless, present policy

---

[1] I develop this argument in my book, *Liberalism*, Milton Keynes and Minneapolis: Open University Press and University of Minnesota Press, 1986, Ch. 6.

cannot be governed simply by the goal of restoring an earlier phase of more limited government. A century and more of interventionism has built up needs and expectations which must be addressed, and it is a mistake to suppose that every move from the *status quo* in the direction of earlier forms of limited government represents an unequivocal improvement. Again, developments wholly external to the growth of government— exogenous changes such as technological innovation and the emergence of a truly global market—render the project of returning to the limited state of early 19th-century England an exercise in anachronism.

We are on firmer ground if instead we take the *status quo* as our point of departure, and ask how government may best be constrained, given the history of the last two hundred years. This involves asking what might be the positive responsibilities of government. In the British tradition, and in Hobbes's theorising of it, the primordial obligation of government is to make and keep peace, where this encompasses forging and maintaining in good repair the institutions of civil society whereby persons and communities with different and incompatible values and per-spectives may co-exist without destructive conflict. It is evident that discharging this duty will commit government to activities that go well beyond the provision of the public goods of national defence and law and order. It may (as I shall later maintain in greater detail) entail government supplying families and com-munities with the means whereby their distinctive values and ways of life may be affirmed and renewed across the generations.

Again, the legal framework of a limited government cannot be (as it might be, if theories of the minimum state were credible) fixed and unalterable. As technology develops and social conditions change, the rules, conventions and practices which make up civil society—which specify the terms of contractual liberty, the character of property rights and the forms of market competition—are bound to require amendment and alteration.

Yet again, the renewal of civil society demands more from government than patient attention to the rules of the game of the market. It requires concern for the health of the autonomous and intermediary institutions which stand between the individual and the state—trade unions, universities, professional organ-isations and the like. Wise legislators (if such we had) would have the responsibility of maintaining what Burke called 'a balanced constitution' by at once ensuring that none of these autonomous

[22]

institutions becomes inordinate in its demands and at the same time assuring them all a protected sphere of independence under the rule of law.

Finally, the conception of the minimum state neglects the crucial questions of membership and allegiance. Who is to be a subject of the minimum state, and how is its jurisdiction to be demarcated? And how could a minimum state command the loyalty of its subjects in time of war? These are questions which classical liberal thought passes over or suppresses, but which are salient to any defensible conception of the modern state.[1]

The Limits of Constitutionalism

The insufficiency of the minimum state is patent. Far less obvious is the danger of relying primarily on constitutionalism as a panacea for our ills. I do not mean by this that we cannot benefit by devising new constitutional conventions. On the contrary, I shall suggest, there are indeed new constitutional devices which we might profitably adopt. The danger to which I refer is rather in supposing that we can at a single stroke cut government down to size by removing personal liberty, and especially the economic dimensions of personal liberty, from the realm of political contestation and embedding it in constitutional law. The ideal of curbing the political domain and enhancing the scope of law, in the belief that individual liberty might thereby be better secured, is a captivating one that has charmed many liberal thinkers. It is nevertheless a snare and a delusion for anyone who seeks to diminish the threat to liberty in Britain today.

That constitutional law, in and of itself, gives insubstantial protection to individual liberty, and fails when it is most needed, is clear enough when we consider recent history. The Constitution of the USSR must be one of the most impressive ever to be conceived, but it counts for little or nothing in the Soviet Union because of the lack of an independent judiciary and the overwhelming concentration of power in the Communist Party. The Soviet example should teach us that, more than upon the terms or provisions of any constitution, individual liberty depends on the dispersion of power through autonomous institutions and society at large.

[1] I considered these questions in the context of a revised version of the liberal conception of the state in my Latham Memorial Lecture, 'The politics of cultural diversity', at the University of Sydney, Australia, in September 1987. The text of this lecture was published in *Quadrant*, November 1987, and an abridged version appears in *The Salisbury Review*, Winter 1988.

The Soviet example is, of course, an extreme one in that it instances a totalitarian state which from its inception has been animated by the project of destroying or repressing the institutions of civil society. In Latin America, and in post-colonial Africa, however, where totalitarian régimes are not yet firmly established, there is many an example of an admirable constitution whose lifespan is limited by the brevity of the régime which gave it birth. This should teach us a second lesson—that the efficacy of a constitution depends critically on the stability of the distribution of power which undergirds it. And that suggests a final, and more comprehensive, observation—that the efficacy of a constitution in protecting individual liberty depends not only on the distribution of economic and political power, but also on the political culture of the people it is meant to safeguard. No constitution will thrive or even take root, if the soil in which it is planted is that of a tyrannous or barbarous political culture.

principally?

Limitations of Constitutional Safeguards

In fact, we need not leave the English-speaking world to see the delusiveness of relying on constitutional provisions as the principal guardians of individual liberty. The paradigm case of the United States is deeply instructive in this regard. The American constitution was deliberately designed to fragment governmental power, restrain majoritarian democracy and protect the necessary conditions of freedom and enterprise. Its early framers and theorists generated constitutionalist insights, which remain valuable today—above all, those of James Madison, who saw that no Bill of Rights could enumerate exhaustively the liberties of the individual (an insight embodied in the Ninth Amendment). Further, the Constitution provided an indispensable framework within which a country of immigrants could develop a national political culture. Its achievements in limiting government over a century and a half in America should never be underestimated. Over the past fifty years, however, it has proved a poor protection against inordinacy in government. For, despite the manifest intentions of its framers, the American Constitution has in many important areas allowed worse invasions of individual liberty than have occurred in many other Western states. We need only think of anti-trust legislation, of the over-regulation of industry, especially of banking, finance and pharmaceuticals, of occupational

It has been more progressive. US would still have legal segregation without it!

[24]

now (1991) being overhauled by Bush

hardly self-evident

licensure, of environmentalist legislation, of many decades of protectionism, of the far-reaching powers of the Internal Revenue Service and of the myriad attempts made by government, at both federal and state level, to enforce paternalist and moralist laws (of which Prohibition is only the most obvious instance) to see that the Constitution has not prevented legislators from making greater inroads into individual liberty in the United States than in many other Western countries.

The case is in practice worse than this. For in the United States, issues—such as abortion, the interests of ethnic and cultural minorities and of women—which elsewhere are resolved by ordinary political reasoning, by mutual accommodation and the political arts, are treated as issues of constitutional law and of basic rights. The result of this process has not been the containment of the political realm but instead the politicisation of law. In consequence, questionable and often plainly unjustified policies of affirmative action, for example, which in other states are matters of legislation whose content is open to political debate, have in the United States become embedded in law at its highest and least alterable levels.

Finally, the separation of powers, which is a cornerstone of the American Constitution, has progressively enfeebled the office of the Presidency and goes far to account for the limitations of the Reagan administration, in which the need to bargain with a refractory and fragmented legislature inhibited the making of hard choices in many areas of policy, and, above all, in respect of the federal deficit. The economic pre-eminence of the United States in the post-war world is owed not to its Constitution, but to the entrepreneurial genius of its people and to the individualist character of its culture. There are, doubtless, important reforms in the US Constitution which might be hoped to return it to the intentions of its framers, but such reforms have little relevance in Britain. In general, the experience of the United States gives small comfort to those in Britain who imagine that the adoption of a written constitution is the best answer to the dilemmas generated by an over-mighty government.

The Failure of the Canadian Constitution and the Treaty of Rome

If there were any reasonable doubt as to this conclusion, it would be dissipated by the evidence of the recent Canadian constitution, in which many of the fads and fallacies of our time—such as the elevation of minority interests to entrenched legal

[25]

[handwritten annotations: "?" at top; "or not!" in right margin; "that's a new one!" in right margin; "resources, technology, war?" in right margin; "It does not have a single document" in right margin; "which has promoted a highly decentralized society where provincial govts. retain all residual powers (contrary to the 'word' of the Constitution)" at bottom]

privileges and all the apparatus of affirmative action— have been carved in stone in the tablets of constitutional law. This is indeed the inexorable result of any uncritical recourse to constitutional-ism at the present time—that it will freeze for perpetuity our cur-rent confusions. Nor is it at all likely that economic liberties— supposing them to be written into a new constitution, which given the current intellectual and political climate is inherently implausible—would be effectively protected by a written constitution.

Doubt as to the efficacy of constitutionalism as the principal guarantor of liberty is turned into certainty when we consider the results of the Treaty of Rome, whose manifest intent of protecting economic freedom has been subverted in practice at many crucial points. If an economic Bill of Rights were enacted in Britain which entrenched liberties of enterprise, contract, trade and property, it would survive only so long as it was not challenged by a majority in Parliament. A conflict between the Commons, say, and whichever body interpreted or adjudicated the terms of an economic Bill of Rights, could only trigger a constitutional crisis in which the constitution as a whole, and thereby the stability of the entire political system, would be likely to be weakened, and our existing liberties endangered.

All this is on the supposition that we are in a position to specify the personal and economic liberties which the consti-tution seeks to protect, which is far from being evident. Many issues of personal liberty—such as those raised by the legal control of immigration, of pornography and narcotics—are matters of legitimate disagreement among reasonable people who are concerned with individual liberty. They are appro-priately dealt with in detailed legislation which expresses a compromise between conflicting interests and values rather than by judicial interpretation of a fixed constitution.

Again, many proposals for an economic Bill of Rights presuppose a liberal world order which no longer exists and which will not be recreated in any foreseeable future. Proposals to entrench a constitutional right to free trade, for example, neglect the vital fact that trade between free economies and totalitarian states, although it may carry with it the classical economic benefits of free trade, nevertheless, by strengthening the economies of the communist states, may harm the cause of liberty. Thus, in terms of domestic political life, in which powerful socialist and interventionist movements would relent-

[26]

lessly contest it, and also in international terms where it would need to be severely qualified in virtue of the rise of totalitarian states, an economic Bill of Rights is a non-starter. And in the absence of these conditions it is probably unnecessary.

The necessary conditions of individual freedom are, in truth, 'constitutional' only in the broadest sense of that term, the sense in which it is employed by Burke. They are delineated most concisely by Michael Oakeshott, when he writes:

'What, then, are the characteristics of our society in respect of which we consider ourselves to enjoy freedom and in default of which we would not be free in our sense of the word? But first, it must be observed that the freedom we enjoy is not composed of a number of independent characteristics of our society which in aggregate make up our liberty. Liberties, it is true, may be distinguished, and some may be more general or more settled and mature than others, but the freedom which the English libertarian knows and values lies in a coherence of mutually supporting liberties, each of which amplifies the whole and none of which stands alone. It springs neither from the separation of church and state, nor from the rule of law, nor from private property, nor from parliamentary government, nor from the writ of *habeas corpus*, nor from the independence of the judiciary, nor from any one of the thousand other devices and arrangements characteristic of our society, but from what each signifies and represents, namely, the absence from our society of overwhelming concentration of power.

'Similarly, the conduct of government in our society involves a sharing of power, not only between the recognised organs of government, but also between the Administration and the Opposition. In short, we consider ourselves to be free because no one in our society is allowed unlimited power—no leader, faction, *debatable* party or 'class', no majority, no government, church, corporation, trade or professional association or trade union. The secret of its freedom is that it is composed of a multitude of organisations in the constitution of the best of which is reproduced that diffusion of power which is characteristic of the whole.'[1]

The Importance of the Constitutional Outlook

Nothing in my criticism of constitutionalist illusion is intended to deny that there are significant constitutional measures which would serve the cause of individual liberty in Britain today. Several examples could be cited, but I will confine myself to four. An amendment requiring that tax allowances be raised in

[1] Oakeshott (1962), *op. cit.*, pp. 40-41.

line with inflation (of the sort promoted under the Rooker-Wise indexation proposals)[1] has an important role in inhibiting the process whereby government pre-empts by stealth an ever greater proportion of the national income.

Again, but more radically, we might envisage a legislative measure which would require government to balance its budget—a measure of the sort proposed in the United States by James Buchanan and others. Such a measure would have the effect, if it could be implemented, of partially restoring that tacit bipartisan economic constitution, respected by Labour Ministers such as Philip Snowden, which it was the work of Keynesianism to overthrow.

A third measure is yet more radical—one requiring that government preserve a stable value in the currency. (I will return later to the question of how this might best be achieved—by the monetarist prescription of a fixed rule for monetary policy or the Hayekian proposal of monetary privatisation and currency competition.) and banks going bust?

A fourth measure might be the incorporation into British law of the European Convention on Human Rights (to which we are, of course, already signatories)—a measure supported by the fact that the rights protected in the Convention are substantially those of classical liberal thought and practice and have proved helpful in curbing the over-mighty powers of trade unions and government bureaucracies.

I am far from underestimating the practical and the potential difficulties of implementing such constitutional measures in Britain. Nor do I intend to comment on the detailed content of such measures—a task beyond the author's competence. At this point, I stress only that measures of a 'constitutional' sort— constitutional in the sense that they aim to institute a framework of rules, conventions or procedures by which the policies of governments of any party are to be constrained—are not only a desirable, but even an indispensable condition, of reviving the project of limited government in Britain. No party at present is committed, clearly and unequivocally, to long-term policies of fiscal conservatism and monetary stability. Even if the present Government were so committed, we could not rest content with a situation in which a single party has a monopoly on these

---

[1] The so-called Rooker-Wise amendment (named after the two Labour Party MPs who tabled it) is a statutory requirement to uprate UK personal tax allowances in line with changes in the Retail Prices Index, i.e. allowing for inflation. It was first enacted in the Finance Act 1977 and was later revised and expanded in the 1980 Finance Act.

[28]

concerns. We have therefore no alternative to pressing on with the task of persuading the major parties that, whereas a fixed constitution or economic Bill of Rights has little or nothing to offer us, we all stand to benefit by forging and adhering to constitutional conventions which restrain the discretionary authority of government economic policy. In other words, we must persuade the major parties of the importance of adopting what James Buchanan has called *a constitutional mentality* in respect of economic policy.

The New Hobbesian Dilemma

I do not seek to disguise the magnitude of the transformation in existing political attitudes, policies and practices presupposed by the adoption of constitutional conventions of the sort I have sketched. It involves a metamorphosis in the character of the modern state as it is found in Britain today that is little short of revolutionary. For consider the stark contrast between the state as Hobbes conceived of it and a modern state such as ours. The state as Hobbes conceived of it had no resources of its own. Its duty in respect of property was exhausted when it had specified the rules for its acquisition and transfer and instituted procedures for arbitrating disputes about it. The Hobbesian state was not (as we have seen) a minimum state of the doctrinaire sort theorised in the writings of Spencer[1] and Nozick[2] and its tasks were not to protect an imaginary set of abstract (and contentless) natural rights. It had tasks above and beyond the provision of law and national defence, including charitable works and an early version of workfare, but its interventions in economic life were strictly limited. Certainly the Hobbesian state is not conceived of as being itself an economic enterprise.

The contrast with a modern state such as ours could not be clearer. The modern British state, like practically every other modern state, owns vast assets (notwithstanding recent exercises in privatisation). At present levels of taxation and expenditure, something between a third and a half of national income is pre-empted by government. Furthermore, the modern British state, again like virtually every other modern state, operates a colossal apparatus of income transfers via progressive taxation, welfare payments, and a welter of tariffs and subsidies. As a result of its

---

[1] For Herbert Spencer's systematic exposition of his political philosophy, see his *The Principles of Ethics*, two vols., Indianapolis: Liberty Press, 1978.

[2] See Robert Nozick, *Anarchy, State and Utopia*, Oxford: Basil Blackwell, 1974.

tremendous economic power, the modern British state continues to exercise an invasive influence on social life of a sort only comparable to that of the absolutist monarchies of early modern Europe. It is perhaps worth remarking that, by virtue of the current burden of taxation, government in Britain today expropriates more of the income and wealth of its subjects than did the lords of feudal times (who were often restricted to command over only one in three of their serfs's labour). And it is worth repeating the point that, on most measures, *the burden of taxation in Britain has increased after a decade of Thatcherism, while the proportion of national income pre-empted by government has not significantly decreased.* (Note redistribution of expenditures)

The consequences of the growth of the state as an owner and controller of great assets with a stake in every aspect of enterprise are large indeed. In a context of mass democracy, it will almost invariably be in the interest of political élites to confer resources on existing and nascent interest groups rather than to reduce or do away with subsidies to them, since the loss to concentrated and collusive groups will always be more politically significant than corresponding benefits to groups that are dispersed. In the modern British state, accordingly, government tends overwhelmingly to service private interests rather than to protect the common good. Contrary to the classical (and Hobbesian) theory of the state as the provider of public goods, *the modern British state is first and foremost a supplier of private goods*. Whereas in the Hobbesian conception, government exists to supply the public good of civil peace, the modern British state exists primarily to satisfy the private preferences of collusive interest groups. A prime example is that of agricultural policy, in which farmers have for decades colluded with civil servants to mould policy according to their interests as producers, but many other instances could be adduced of the transformation of government from a provider of public goods into an engine for the promotion of private interests. In suffering this metamorphosis, government has defaulted on its classical functions of defending the realm, keeping the peace and renewing and repairing the institutions of civil society.

The Waning of Civil Society

As government has waxed, so civil society has waned. This is the mutation in our circumstances identified in Hayek's *The Road to Serfdom*. The result in contemporary Britain of the erosion of

[30]

civil society by an expansionist state has been the eruption of a *was it ever?* *political struggle for resources.* From being an umpire which enforces the rules of the game of civil association, the *British state has become the most powerful weapon in an incessant competition for resources.* Its power is sought by every interest and enterprise, partly because of the huge assets it already owns or controls, but also because no private or corporate asset is safe from invasion or confiscatory taxation. From being a contrivance whereby the peaceful co-existence of civil association is assured, the state has itself become an instrument of predation, whereby a political war of all against all is fought. Civil life soon comes to resemble the Hobbesian state of nature from which it was meant to deliver us. The Hobbesian state is the classical solution of the Prisoners' Dilemma[1] faced by all in the state of nature: each must pre-emptively seek power over the rest, if only to defend himself from attack. By providing a legal framework, coercively enforced, the Hobbesian state releases its subjects from destructive conflict into the peace and commodious living of civil society.

In the modern British state this order of things has been reversed. Individuals and enterprises are constrained to organise collusively so as to capture or colonise the interventionist state. As a result, productive energies are distracted into the struggle for influence in government. So is generated *the new Hobbesian dilemma*, in which subjects are constrained, often solely in self-defence, to expend their energies in capturing or colonising government institutions, in seeking influence over government policy, in order to protect or promote their interests against others—typically other producer groups—who are similarly constrained. The result is the legal war of all against all, with the Prisoners' Dilemma of the state of nature being reproduced in the context of an over-extended government and a weak civil society.

? Is a State ever distinct from society

The nemesis of this process, which we are mercifully far from confronting at present, can only be an impoverishment of civil society and the recreation of the state of nature by political means. The example of Peronist Argentina suggests that once this process has occurred, it is difficult, perhaps impossible, to reverse it—as the recent election to the presidency of Argentina of the Peronist Carlos Menem confirms. In Britain, we need

---

[1] The Prisoners' Dilemma, and the Hobbesian state as the solution to the public goods trap which the Dilemma generates, are brilliantly set out and assessed in Anthony de Jasay's *Social Contract, Free Ride*, Oxford: Basil Blackwell, 1989.

think only of the later years of the last Labour Government to see that it would be complacency to suppose that we are immune from this new Hobbesian dilemma. Indeed, it is the burden of my argument that, contrary to its professed intentions, the present Government is abandoning the project of a limited state, and in arrogating to itself ever more discretionary powers, is creating the machinery through which a new political struggle for resources is bound to be fought. What is to be done?

Public Goods and Market Competition

The first and most essential step is the recognition that government activity should be confined to the production of public goods. In a Hobbesian perspective, the greatest of these is peace, but the pursuit of peace involves government in the provision of goods that go well beyond those comprehended in the maintenance of law and order. As I shall argue later, the concern by government for a civil society that is free from destructive conflict should lead it to a concern with the distribution (and not just the efficient production) of wealth, since a society with a substantial propertyless underclass cannot reasonably be expected to be stable when the resentments of those with nothing are open to exploitation by radical movements. In addition to such involvements by government as are imposed upon it by its task of keeping the peace and superintending civil society, government may legitimately act to provide a variety of other public goods. Here I do not intend to specify as public only those goods which in the strict economic theory of the subject are indivisible and non-excludable, so that they are either produced by government or not at all, but instead any good which has weighty positive 'externalities'.

Universal literacy, for example, whatever disadvantages it may have, is a benefit to everyone in society, and government may legitimately act to promote it. Similarly, though more controversially, common cultural traditions provide the matrix without which the exercise by individuals of their autonomy becomes impoverished and attenuated, and government may act to promote the common culture by the support of the arts and by other measures. Here we may mention an important maxim, the first among several we shall invoke for the restraint of government:

Government may act to provide a public good so long as the coercive aspect of such action is confined to its financing from taxation and the provision of the

[32]

good by government does not tend to monopolise or dominate any market which may exist in that good.

As Hayek has well stated this maxim: *Smith's Lighthouses*

'Insofar as government merely undertakes to supply societies which otherwise would not be supplied at all (usually because it is not possible to confine the benefits to those prepared to pay for them), the only question which arises is whether the benefits are worth the cost. Of course, if the government claimed for itself the exclusive right to provide particular services, they would cease to be strictly non-coercive. In general, a free society demands not only that the government have a monopoly of coercion but that it have the monopoly only of coercion and that in all other respects it operate on the same terms as everybody else.'[1]

Hayek's maxim, which echoes J. S. Mill's distinction between the 'authoritative' and 'non-authoritative' activities of government (according to which government may provide any public goods so long as the coercion involved is restricted to taxation), requires not only that the state claim no monopolistic power in respect of its provision of the good, but also that its action should not dominate the market in it so as to swamp all private initiative in its provision. By this criterion, state support for the arts may be legitimate, but the present near-monopoly in schooling is not. The maxim we have enumerated has a corollary which is also worth mentioning. This is that policy should be guided by the aim that, aside no doubt from the core services of national defence and law enforcement, *government should, so far as is possible, always be constrained in its activities by market competition.* As we shall see, this is a maxim with far-reaching and sometimes radical implications.

The Ethics of Market Freedom

But what is the moral justification of relying so heavily on market competition? What, in other words, is the ethical argument for market freedom?

In classical liberal writings, market freedom and its precondition, private property, are often defended negatively, as shields against coercion by other men or by a tyrannous state. This is, at best, only half of the story. The most fundamental argument for market freedom is in its contribution to individual wellbeing by positively enabling people to act in pursuit of their

---

[1] F. A. Hayek, *The Constitution of Liberty*, Chicago: Henry Regnery, 1960, pp. 222-23.

goals and to express their values and ideals. Unlike any collective decision-procedure, howsoever democratic, the market enables individuals to act to achieve their ends without the necessity of consulting their fellows, a procedure which often occasions social conflict, where it does not result in majoritarian tyranny. The market provides the positive freedom of autonomy and self-determination, accordingly, and not only the negative freedom of non-interference. Where, as with us, human values and goals are indefinitely various, and society harbours a diversity of cultural traditions and conceptions of the good life, market provision of most goods is a condition of peace, since each may act with his own resources to achieve the good without thereby depleting any collective resource. But the market not only allows practitioners of different traditions and proponents of different values to live together in peaceful co-existence, it also enables new values to appear and new minorities to form. As Hayek put it:

'... action by collective agreement limited to measures where previous efforts have already created a common view, where opinion about what is desirable has become settled, and where the problem is that of choosing between possibilities already generally recognised, not that of discovering new possibilities. Public opinion, however, cannot decide in what direction efforts should be made to arouse public opinion, and neither government nor other existing organised groups should have the exclusive power to do so. But organised efforts have to be set in motion by a few individuals who possess the necessary resources themselves or who win the support of those that do; without such men, what are now the views of a small minority may never have a chance of being adopted by the majority.'[1]

The ethical argument for the market is, then, not only that it allows practitioners of different traditions and values to live in peaceful co-existence, but also that it allows for innovation and novelty in thought and practice in a way that collective decisions cannot. This is to say that market freedom protects the very basic freedom to think new thoughts and try out new practices. At its most fundamental, the moral argument for the free market is one that appeals to its indispensable role in *enabling* people to implement their ideas and realise their goals. The language of 'enablement' is particularly apt, since it has lately been co-opted

[1] Hayek, *ibid.*, p. 126.

by critics of the market. Such critics do not (or will not) see that it is only the institutions of the market that accord full respect to human agency, while efforts to 'empower' people through government intervention typically turn them into passive consumers of impersonal bureaucracies.

The Market Is Indispensable to Liberty

The justification of the market is, in the end, then, as an indispensable condition of autonomy and self-determination. The claim that free markets best achieve prosperity, like the claim that markets allocate scarce resources most efficiently, though true, is not fundamental. Again, Adam Smith's famous observation that we rely on the self-interest, and not the benevolence, of the butcher for our provisions, does not go to the bottom of things, despite its being indisputably correct. The case for the market is not that it allows for the motive of self-interest—for who supposes that motive to be absent when resources are subject to collective, political allocation?—but that it allows for the whole variety of human motives, in all their complexity and mixtures. The defence of the market goes astray, accordingly, when it represents it as a means to aggregate social welfare. Instead, we should see the ethical standing of the market in its respect for human agency and its contribution to human autonomy.

In order to participate fully in the free market, people sometimes need resources the market has not conferred on them. It is for that reason that a limited government, committed to the market economy, may and often ought to act to provide those with small resources with the wherewithal to make good use of market freedoms. When government so acts, it does so in accordance with the maxim that *a necessary background condition of a stable market order is a wide diffusion of wealth and a reasonable measure of equality of opportunity*. That this is no empty banality will become clear when we come to consider its implications for the tax treatment of savings and inheritance and the distributional aspects of voucher, loan and negative income tax schemes. However a limited government acts to confer resources and opportunities on those who have hitherto had few assets or options, it best prepares people for responsible life in a market economy by using the institutions of the market itself. It is for this reason that, when government acts to provide an underproduced public good, or to correct distributional anomalies, it

OVER
→

[35]

should do so, in most contexts, by providing purchasing power and not by the direct provision of goods or services. It thereby conforms to the maxim that *markets are best reformed by the further development of markets.*

III. POLICY

'The practical moral of the failure of both the Reagan and
Thatcher attempts to cut the public spending ratio is the futility of
trying to roll back public expenditure without fundamental
changes in the agenda of government.'

SAMUEL BRITTAN[1]

No set of legal or constitutional devices can by themselves
restore limited government. Our best prospect is in a range of
measures which dismantle or restructure interventionist restric-
tions and policies and reshape the environment in which
enterprise operates. Our objective is so to strengthen the
autonomous institutions of civil life that (as in 19th-century
England) the government is effectively constrained by the
countervailing powers of independent social forces.

I will consider the measures which seem to be appropriate
under four heads: first, the monetary framework of enterprise;
second, the privatisation of the welfare state; third, the role of
intermediary institutions and of local authorities; and fourth and
last, but certainly not least, the legitimate distributional concerns
and activities of a limited government in Britain. In the course of
this exploration, I shall consider the role of government in
education, the moral and cultural conditions of the free market,
and several other issues where prevailing opinion appears to be
at odds with the ideal of limited government.

1. THE FRAMEWORK OF GOVERNMENT

A. Monetary Stability

I observed earlier that a vital obligation of the state (on which
almost all modern states, including the present British Government, have defaulted) is the maintenance of a stable currency.
The crux of the present dilemma is that money is everywhere
(even in states with a central bank having a measure of real
independence) under the arbitrary control of governments
subject to the vicissitudes of ephemeral political circumstances

---

[1] Samuel Brittan, *A Restatement of Economic Liberalism*, London: Macmillan, 1988, p. 249.

and governed by the vote motive. Given the costs and pains inseparable from a policy which genuinely aims at a zero inflation rate, it is inevitable that modern democratic government (except in Germany and Japan, where special historical factors and central banks with strong regulatory powers are important) should have a built-in inflationist bias.

The dilemma of a policy for stable money goes yet deeper than this. The unprecedented prosperity of the Liberal Era—the century between the Napoleonic Wars and the First World War—owed much to the stability provided by the impersonal and politically largely untouchable mechanism of the gold standard. Economic fluctuations occurred, but they were typically sharp and brief. Even with the demise of the gold standard between the Wars, post-war reconstruction brought about another guarantor of international monetary stability in the Bretton Woods system of fixed exchange rates. The breakdown of this system was predictable and unavoidable, given the very different inflation rates prevailing in the various Western economies, with Britain from the Sixties onwards being the leader of the baleful process of currency debasement. A system of floating rates was then irresistible, but it has signally failed to satisfy the expectations of those who then championed it and has fully justified the Cassandra-like warnings of Hayek, who always opposed it. Rates of exchange are now volatile to a degree which infects business enterprise with a speculative psychology. Further, the ending of exchange controls (in itself an eminently desirable measure, and one of the high watermarks of policy under the Thatcher administration) has made the control by government of the total supply of money even more difficult. Policies of currency management by target zones or other devices are at best temporary expedients.

Our dilemma is indeed so difficult that Hayek has been driven to the extreme of advocating currency competition as the only effective way of disciplining government fiat monies. His radical proposal[1] that the governmental monopoly on money issuance be ended and private monies, subject to market disciplines, be allowed to emerge, has, I shall argue, many decisive advantages over the monetarist prescription that the control of money by government be constrained by fixed rules.

Hayek's proposal is one that will be regarded by mainstream

[1] F. A. Hayek, *Denationalisation of Money—The Argument Refined*, Hobart Paper 70, London: Institute of Economic Affairs, 2nd edn., 1978.

opinion among economists and politicians as in the realm of the politically impossible, but it will be the upshot of my argument that a lasting release from the uncertainty of endemic inflation is, in fact, to be expected only from radical measures of precisely the sort that appear at present to be politically impossible.

The Morality of Monetarism

If by 'monetarism' we mean here the proposition that stable overall prices are a vital part of the framework of enterprise in a free society, then monetarism so understood has clear foundations in ordinary morality. Its justification is not in the economic growth stable money ordinarily facilitates, but in the moral hazards of inflation. (I set aside here the parallel dangers of *deflation*, since in the period from the end of the Second World War until the present, at any rate, the prospect of a general deflation has been far more remote than that of an endemic inflation.)

Chronic inflation has a corrosive impact on social and individual morality in a variety of ways. In the first place it results typically in a continuous redistribution of resources from civil society to government, since in most countries tax allowances are not subject to indexation against the rising price level, and taxpayers are therefore subject to the unremitting confiscatory pressure of fiscal drag. This is a process which undermines individual responsibility by making the real, post-tax income of the individual a function not of his efforts at prudence but of a vast impersonal process over which he can exercise little or no control.

Further, the impact of inflation varies radically, and often inequitably, across society. Those with substantial real assets in property or equities, for example, are usually able to protect themselves, while those dependent on fixed incomes are powerless, and the majority that relies on income from earnings is likely to be locked in constant conflict with employers. Debtors are rewarded and savers punished. Inflation thereby acts so as to effect an arbitrary and morally objectionable redistribution of resources across society. Again, the prospect of continuing inflation makes people reluctant to provide for their old age.

In an inflationary economy, people will look to government as the only power capable of protecting them from evils of which government itself is the chief cause. The result is an inescapable

[39]

tendency towards further expansion in the size and inter-ventionist activity of government. There is, last in the list of the moral hazards of inflation, its corrupting effect on the ethics of contractual exchange. In an inflationary environment, contractual exchange faces not only the ordinary risks and uncertainties of market valuation, but also the larger insecurity generated by currency debasement at unpredictable rates.

It is, perhaps, worth making once again the classical point that the success of inflationist policies depends crucially on the persistence of a pre-inflationary psychology—in short, on money illusion. Once people are cured by persistent doses of inflationary policy of their money illusion, and so come to index their expectations, the stimulating effect of monetary laxity on the economy begins to be lost. Inflationary policy is therefore self-limiting, and indeed self-defeating, in its effects over the medium run of a generation or so. It is not facetious to observe that the success of a 'Keynesian' policy of loose money depends on the existence of a majority of 'pre-Keynesian' people, which it is the effect of 'Keynesian' policy to destroy.

If human expectations under inflation soon come to be 'indexed', why not index contracts, so hoping to nullify the deleterious effects of inflation? Indexation of contracts, the inclusion of escalator clauses specifying the terms of exchange in real rather than nominal values, may offer some short-term protection to individuals, but it serves further to disco-ordinate *relative* prices and so make the task of the producer, entrepreneur and investor harder. In theory, it is true, perfect indexation of all prices would make relative prices transparent and, in effect, simulate price stability. In practice, since not all prices will be indexed and the indices of inflation used will themselves be far from perfect, the effect of indexation is to further distort the real economy. Indexation is thus not even a second-best to stable money, which is the only way of avoiding the moral hazards of inflation.

The ultimate justification of 'monetarism' as the project for ending inflation is not then in its contribution to economic growth, but in the moral hazards of inflation. It is equity, and not the claims of general welfare, that is most immediately imperilled by chronic inflation. But what of monetarism as a prescription for policy?

[40]

B. The Monetarist Project Defined and Assessed

Understood as the morality of sound money, monetarism is unimpeachable. As a set of policy prescriptions, it is much more questionable. Essentially, monetarism as a project in policy-making holds that the object of stable prices is most likely to be achieved by government control of the money stock according to fixed and known rules. In Britain, this was the view embodied in the Medium-Term Financial Strategy, and in the United States, Milton Friedman and others have urged that the Federal Reserve be constrained in its activity by strict rules regarding the quantity of money to be issued. In favour of monetarism as a policy prescription, it must be affirmed that the monetarist critique of the discretionary authority of central banks and governments over the money supply is thoroughly supported by evidence. Indeed, one of the strongest parts of the monetarist case is the claim that the discretionary action of central banks has been responsible for some of the most serious economic dislocations, such as the Great Depression, where it has been convincingly argued that an excessive reduction in the money stock triggered a decline in economic activity that turned recession into collapse.[1]

The monetarist solution—of holding central banks to fixed rules—faces difficulties, however, that in all probability are insoluble. There is, first, an *a priori* point about the systematic elusiveness of money in a complex modern economy. As Hayek has always emphasised, 'money' in modern economies is not a single or a simple phenomenon, but an attribute of many financial instruments and practices. Like other social objects, money is subjective—it is constituted by the beliefs and expectations people have about it.

These, rather recondite, considerations perhaps had little practical significance for policy prior to the deregulation of financial institutions, and could safely be ignored. In present circumstances, however, they have considerable practical force. The abolition of exchange controls, and the ever-increasing internationalisation of credit, have opened the British economy to flows of money that cannot be controlled by domestic monetary policy. Financial deregulation further deepens the problem. Now that building societies and other institutions act

---

[1] For an argument to this conclusion, see M. Friedman and A.J. Schwartz, *A Monetary History of the United States, 1867-1960*, Princeton: Princeton University Press, 1963.

like banks in creating credit, money is, in effect, being generated by a host of institutions not subject to significant governmental control. This means that the theoretical difficulties in measuring and controlling the money supply theorised by Hayek have in considerable measure become practical realities and make the monetarist solution increasingly unreal and anachronistic.

It will be objected by monetarists (such as Congdon)[1] that these considerations fail to account for the comparative success of monetarist policy in Britain between 1979 and 1985. On this monetarist analysis, the rising trend in inflation since late 1985 is simply the result of a policy reversal in which monetary control was abandoned and laxity in the money supply allowed. Considered as an historical interpretation of the actual course of events, this monetarist analysis may well be sound. Using various measures of broad money, Congdon was himself able, uniquely, to predict the inflation of the past year or so. But, even if such measurement and prediction is achievable, it is more than doubtful whether control of the total money supply can be achieved in current circumstances. On the analysis presented here, monetarist policy would have become increasingly unworkable after 1985 even if there had not been the policy reversal hypothesised by Congdon. In general, it seems that successful monetarist policy is incompatible with extensive financial deregulation, and can be revived only by reimposition of a corset of controls on financial institutions, including possibly exchange controls—a prospect that is probably unrealisable and certainly undesirable.

There are, in addition to these difficulties, serious problems for monetarist policy of a political and constitutional sort. Even if the monetarist analysis of the period 1979-85 be correct, the fact would remain that monetary policies shifted at that time and the earlier policy was junked. In a public choice perspective, such policy reversals are inevitable in the context of a mass democracy in which governments are subject to the recurrent

---

[1] See Tim Congdon's excellent article in *Economic Affairs*, Vol. 8, No. 3, February/March 1988, pp. 14-18, 'The Lawson Boom in the Light of the Crash'. I would like to express my view that, whereas Congdon's positions both on methodology and policy in monetary matters are ones I reject on Hayekian grounds, his achievement in predicting the current inflation, almost alone among practising economists in Britain, is extraordinary and deserving of wider recognition. Rising inflation and interest rates in mid-1989 have further strengthened Congdon's historical analysis, which he has set out systematically in *Monetarism Lost: and Why it Must be Regained*, Centre for Policy Studies, May 1989.

pressure of the vote motive and the collusive pressures of interest groups. As developed by the Virginia School, and especially by James Buchanan and Gordon Tullock,[1] the public choice perspective views the behaviour of politicians and bureaucrats as governed by the same imperatives as rule the consumer and producer in the market. In this economic interpretation of political life, it is to be expected that a monetarist anti-inflation strategy will not survive the long haul of political competition. There appears to be an insuperable political obstacle to monetarist policy, then, which is evidenced by the very policy reversal Congdon and others maintain occurred in 1985. So what is to be done?

The Difficulties of a Monetary Constitution

Within the Virginia School of Public Choice itself, it has been proposed that the monetary activities of government be constrained by strict rules. Thus Buchanan and Brennan have suggested[2] the imposition of a régime of rules on the governmental monetary authority—the constitutionalisation of monetary policy, in effect. But this proposal confronts very powerful objections, stated concisely by Kevin Dowd in his Hobart Paper, *Private Money*:

> 'To begin with, such rules could easily destabilise the banking system still further. A classic example of a potentially destabilising rule would be the abolition of the central banks' lender-of-last-resort function whilst retaining the restrictions on the commercial banks' freedom to issue notes. Since these restrictions give rise to the apparent "need" for a government lender of last resort, such a rule could leave the banking system exposed to a crisis it could not handle.'[3]

Hayek has made a related point:

> 'As regards Professor Friedman's proposal of a legal limit on the rate at which a monopolistic issue of money was to be allowed to increase the quantity in circulation, I can only say that I would like to see what would happen if under such a provision it ever became known that the amount of cash in circulation was approaching the upper

[1] James Buchanan and Gordon Tullock, *The Calculus of Consent*, Michigan: University of Michigan Press, 1962.

[2] James Buchanan and Geoffrey Brennan, *Monopoly in Money and Inflation: The Case for a Constitution to Discipline Government*, Hobart Paper 88, London: IEA, 1981.

[3] Kevin Dowd, *Private Money: The Path to Monetary Stability*, Hobart Paper 112, London: IEA, 1988, pp. 58-59.

limit and that therefore a need for increased liquidity could not be met.'[1]

In support of this observation, Hayek cites Walter Bagehot's classic statement:

'In a sensitive state of the English money market the near approach to the legal limit of reserve would be a sure incentive to panic; if one-third were fixed by law, the moment the banks were close to one-third alarm would begin and would run like magic.'[2]

In this connection, it is fascinating to note that Bagehot himself favoured ideally a system of free banking, but regarded it as impracticable. As he put it in *Lombard Street*:

'. . . the natural system of banking is that of many banks keeping their own cash reserve, with the penalty of failure before them if they neglect it. I have shown that our system is that of a single bank keeping the whole reserve under no effectual penalty of failure. And yet I propose to retain that system, and only attempt to mend and palliate it.

'I can only reply that I propose to retain that system because I am quite sure that it is of no use proposing to alter it . . . You might as well, or better, try to alter the English monarchy and substitute a republic, as to alter the present constitution of the English money market, founded on the Bank of England.'[3]

Correct as Bagehot's judgement may have been when he made it, recent developments suggest it has less plausibility now. One indication of this possibility is the recent conversion of the world's foremost monetarist, Milton Friedman, to a version of free banking. Friedman now advocates radical, non-monetarist measures:

'. . . abolish the money-creating powers of the Federal Reserve, freeze the quality of high-powered money, and deregulate the financial system'.[4]

Friedman's recent proposals are powerful reinforcement to the

[1] Hayek, *Denationalisation of Money*, *op. cit.*, p. 72.

[2] Hayek, *ibid.*, p. 77.

[3] Walter Bagehot, *Lombard Street: A Description of the Money Market* (1904), New York: Arno Press, 1979, pp. 328-29.

[4] Milton Friedman, 'Monetary Policy: Tactics versus Strategy', in J. Dorn and A. J. Schwartz (eds.), *The Search for Stable Money*, Chicago: University of Chicago Press, 1987, p. 381.

view that a monetary constitution confronts insuperable obstacles in the United States.

A monetary constitution is in any case not a feasible remedy for the British problem of sound money. In Britain a monetary constitution could not be entrenched, given parliamentary sovereignty and our unfixed constitution. Further, as Dowd notes, the proposal of a monetary constitution has the disadvantage of retaining a considerable measure of government intervention (and, it may be added, all the classic disadvantages of monopoly). A return to more extensive and discretionary intervention by government in the money supply is a permanent possibility in Britain. The solution of privatising money by allowing for competition among concurrent currencies therefore deserves careful consideration despite its radically innovative aspects.

C. The Case for Currency Competition

The limitations of monetarist policy, and the argument for currency competition as the best achievable constraint on government's monetary activities, were stated programmatically by Samuel Brittan in his Hobart Paper, *How to End the 'Monetarist' Controversy*:

> 'The defects of monetarism, in the narrow sense of the fixed rule for domestic money supply, are that it concedes too much power to official intervention, underrates the influence of competition in providing monetary substitutes, and takes official statistics far too much at their face value. "Friedmanites" are often very good at analysing how controls and regulations in the economy generally will be avoided or will produce unintended effects quite different from those their sponsors desire. But too often they evince a touching faith in government in their own special sphere.

> 'The invention of new monetary instruments to replace old ones— and competition between currencies—is becoming more important as communications improve further and capital markets become even more closely linked. The abolition of exchange control in Britain in 1979 was bound to create complications for the measurement and control of the quantity of money, as the evolution of the Eurodollar market had already done for the USA.

> 'It is upside-down logic to suggest it was therefore wrong to abolish exchange control or reduce barriers between capital markets. The reluctance of people to hold a freely-tradeable worldwide currency

which depreciates rapidly and erratically is a bigger long-run constraint on inflationary policies than monetary targets achieved by controls and manipulations which distort the meaning of the aggregates controlled.'[1]

The implication of Brittan's analysis is that we have already a considerable measure of currency competition in the UK. A natural question then arises: Why has not inflation continued to fall? What accounts for its resurgence in the late 1980s? One answer has to do with the deregulation of financial institutions. As monetarists have themselves observed, the entry of banks into the mortgage market may have triggered a housing-led inflation in which credit was expanded, not only by the banks and the building societies, but also by owner-occupiers taking out home equity loans on the strength of rising house prices. Another, and probably more fundamental, answer is to emphasise the radicalism of Hayek's proposal and the modest degree to which it has been approximated. As Peter Brimelow has observed:

'Hayek's proposal is particularly radical because it combines a number of distinct ideas that are already quite radical enough:

o "Free banking"—banks ought to be able to issue currency and create deposits (conceptually the same thing), choose their own reserve ratios and generally operate entirely without regulation.

o Different denominations—privately issued currencies need not be all denominated in the same unit: Citibank's Wristons and Chase Manhattan's Rockefellers would be traded against each other in a currency market just as the different national currencies are today.

o Private fiat money—these private currencies need not necessarily be convertible into gold or any underlying commodity, but would trade entirely on the word of the issuing bank that it would not debauch its money.'[2]

In combining these three radical proposals, Hayek's scheme takes us into uncharted territory. Nonetheless, the historical parallels we have at our disposal, such as the experiment in free banking in Scotland from 1728 to 1845, should encourage us to explore further Hayek's suggestion. In the British case, implementing it would (as Dowd has made clear) involve abol-

[1] Samuel Brittan, How to End the 'Monetarist' Controversy, Hobart Paper 90, London: IEA, 1981, p. 84.

[2] Peter Brimelow, Forbes, 30 May 1988, p. 246.

ishing the Bank of England, complete financial deregulation and the redefinition of the monetary standard in terms of a general commodity index. No country is at present prepared to countenance such proposals, involving as they do a massive relinquishment of government influence on the economy. Nevertheless, given the manifest failure of other policies, and the ingenuity of deregulated financial institutions in developing products to counteract governmental currency debasement, it may be that the privatisation of money is an idea whose time has come. If this is so, it will support one of the maxims enumerated at the start of this survey—that in our circumstances *government is best constrained in most of its activities by market competition* (rather than by a régime of rules which are typically honoured in the breach).

Advantages of Currency Competition

Currency competition would, it is reasonable to suppose, have many crucial advantages over current practice and over monetarist alternatives. Its chief recommendation is that it offers a promising, albeit a very radical, route to long-term stability in prices, and that it does so by harnessing those very processes of market competition which elsewhere have proved the most reliable guardians of general welfare. We see in the case for currency competition, accordingly, an instance of a paradox which may have more general applications—*that the public good of price stability is best secured by private provision.* We need not suppose that currency competition would have some of the results attributed to it by its supporters, such as a return to the gold standard, or an end to fractional-reserve banking, to see it as the most promising way of cutting the Gordian knot of government-created inflation. Our present circumstance, which approximates Hayek's proposal in that it already evidences semi-free banking and the discipline of comparatively free currency markets, has probably prevented government-induced inflation from being worse than it might otherwise have been. In this present context, anti-inflation policy is best conducted by using the lever of interest rates. In the longer run, however, in which we approximate further the Hayekian régime, governmental control of interest rates is bound to diminish. As Hayek has described the highly desirable return of interest rates to control by market forces:

'With the central banks and the monopoly of the issue of money would, of course, disappear also the possibility of deliberately determining the rate of interest ... The whole idea that the rate of interest ought to be used as an instrument of policy is entirely mistaken, since only competition in a free market can take account of all the circumstances which ought to be taken account of in the determination of the rate of interest.'[1]

The case for currency competition deserves the most serious consideration, if only because (in sharp contrast with monetarism) it does not expect government to succeed in producing the optimum amount of money, when it has signally failed in most other areas.

D. The Framework of Enterprise

As I have argued, the necessary condition of free enterprise is not the minimum state but framework government. I have concentrated on the monetary framework since, more than anything else, it is indispensable to a stable market order. My conclusions have been that government can best secure stable money by privatising (or, at the least, demonopolising) it within a context of free banking. The contribution of limited government to stable money is that of defining the legal framework of free banking. Other aspects of the framework of enterprise are doubtless important—most notably, the legal power of trade unions, whose continued enjoyment of the legal immunities granted them in the 1906 Trade Disputes Act remains a distortion of contractual liberty. Equally, there may be significant areas for constructive reform in company law.

Again, privatisation policy raises important issues in those instances, regrettably so far the majority, where it has been principally a revenue measure and has not been accompanied by significant enhancements in competition. Yet again, the professions remain massively over-regulated, and any policy that favours market freedom must, sooner rather than later, confront the guild socialism of the established professions. I pass over these other topics, since I believe that none of them rivals in importance the need for stable money as a foundation for market freedom.

2. PRIVATISING THE WELFARE STATE

The term 'the Welfare State' designates nothing definite. It embraces such disparate arrangements as state retirement

[1] Hayek, *Denationalisation of Money, op. cit.*, pp. 102-103.

[48]

pensions, maternity and disability benefits, the National Health Service, personal social services, municipal housing, education and unemployment and social security payments. The lack of any precise meaning of the term reflects an underlying lack of theoretical and moral content in the very conception of the welfare state and the historical fact that it has been shaped in its present form not by any genuine consensus on principles but by a succession of contingencies, of which war and the vote motive are the two main categories.

To say this is to say (what is the plain truth) that the welfare state as we know it has no rationale, no animating principle and no genuine justification. It is not an adequate safety net, nor an instrument whereby the underclass is reintegrated into civil life, nor yet an effective machinery for redistribution, but virtually the contrary of each of these distinct institutions. The welfare state does not relieve poverty but institutionalises it. It does not emancipate the underclass but instead imprisons it in ghettoes of dependency (such as municipal housing estates). It does not redistribute income from rich to poor but instead, for the most part, acts in accordance with Director's Law, that is to say, it serves as a middle-class racket whereby income transfers are effected from rich and poor to the majority in the middle. As George Stigler has observed:

> 'Government has coercive power which allows it to engage in acts (above all, the taking of resources) which could not be done by voluntary agreement of all the members of a society. Any portion of society which can secure control of the state's machinery will employ that machinery to improve its own position. Under a set of conditions ... this dominant group will be the middle-income classes. Empirical investigation appears to establish that the necessary conditions for this law are created in the United States through farm policy, minimum wage laws, social security, public housing, public provision for higher education, tax exempt institutions, and "welfare expenditures".
>
> '... Public expenditures are made primarily for the benefit of the middle classes, and financed with taxes which are borne in considerable part by the poor and the rich.'[1]

The welfare state as we know it is a ruleless chaos of cross-subsidies about which there are only two general truths—that, as

---

[1] G. Stigler, 'Director's Law of Public Income Distribution', *Journal of Law and Economics*, April 1970.

Hayekian logic — say it 3 times and it is proven! In truth only saying, "We can imagine situations in which it might be true."

things stand, it is the affluent, leisured, verbally and socially skilled middle classes that do best out of it and that (because of the huge transaction costs, moral hazards and sheer waste associated with it) all, or nearly all, of us would probably be better off if the welfare state had never been invented.

It would nevertheless be folly to suppose that we can somehow simply abolish the welfare state, or to underestimate the massive difficulties in the way of any policy of its radical reform. It would be wrong to attempt simply to abolish the welfare state, not merely because the electoral imperatives of a democratic party render that option politically incredible, but because justice interdicts such a policy. Millions are now dependent on government for all or a major part of their income because earlier unjust policies of inflationary financing and confiscatory taxation deprived them of the opportunity of providing for themselves. Any policy of radical reform by privatisation of the welfare state must face the fact that we will need at least a generation in which to diminish to an in-eliminable minimum the burden of dependency fostered by earlier policies.

Utopian Alternatives:
The Universal Negative Income Tax

We must beware, also, of simplistic alternatives to our present confusion. One of these, which has been much in favour among latter-day classical liberals, egalitarian social democrats and market-oriented conservatives, is the universal negative or reverse income tax, whereby those with little or no income have it automatically supplemented by government up to a point of decent subsistence.

The scheme has the immediate appeal of targeting the neediest and of apparent administrative elegance, but this appeal is almost entirely delusive. In the first place, such a scheme would be a marked improvement on existing arrangements if, but only if, it replaced them altogether. In practice it would not do so, since replacing existing transfers entirely by a negative income tax would inexorably mean that the scheme would either become ruinously expensive or else involve politically costly and conceivably inequitable losses for some groups. In practice, one may confidently predict that the scheme would be tacked on to existing arrangements as a supplement to them— and our last state would be worse than our first.

Even if it could be introduced in all its purity as a full alternative to prevailing institutions, the negative income tax scheme would soon be inflated beyond all recognition. The vote motive would generate a political competition for resources whereby the subsistence level would be progressively bid up, subject only to the constraint imposed by consequent tax rates. It is this practical certainty, rather than real but incidental problems to do with the choice of a tax unit (individuals or families? over what time period?) and with the administration of the scheme, that condemn it.

The public choice analysis pioneered by the Virginia School suggests the overwhelming likelihood that the scheme would in practice rapidly degenerate into a vast late-20th-century Speenhamland system of outdoor poor relief. As Hutt has observed:

> 'If it were "politically possible" for "reverse income tax" to be accepted solely as a substitute for all other forms of electoral vote-buying, the outcome of such a substitution would be a magnificent achievement. It would mean the abandonment of kinds of control of men which curb freedom and are an affront to human dignity. It was largely because of this virtue of his proposal that Professor Friedman was inspired to put forward his scheme (in his great book, *Capitalism and Freedom*). Its adoption on his terms would be welcomed by all concerned about the survival of liberty in a world in which political power-seekers increasingly appease the intolerant. But it would not cease to be a means through which candidates for election would compete in generosity at the expense of taxpayers. And its supporters must openly avow this as a serious calculated risk.

> 'Professor Friedman has made no unjustified claims for his scheme. Yet it so resembles the notorious Speenhamland wage supplement of 1795 that it is impossible not to retain misgivings. The chief merit of the plan is one which he does not himself claim: that it exposes the vote-purchasing incentive for income transfers.'[1]

The Benefits and Hazards of Targeted Voucher and Negative Income Tax Schemes

A universal negative income tax has overwhelming disadvantages. This is not to say that some limited variations on a negative income tax may not be the least bad alternatives to many existing transfers. Child benefit and income support to

[1] W. H. Hutt, *Politically Impossible?*, Hobart Paperback 1, London: Institute of Economic Affairs, 1971, p. 42.

one-parent families (where the absent parent cannot be made to shoulder his obligations) might profitably be turned into limited and targeted reverse income tax schemes. Providing they were not universal in scope, such schemes would have the virtues of maximum selectivity and (at least with marginal tax rates of no more than 50 per cent) of retaining a degree of incentive for the recipients. Unemployment assistance might also conceivably be in the form of a 50/50 negative income tax, where (as may often be the case) workfare schemes prove unworkable. Even in the case of disability assistance, where governments have been niggardly rather than over-generous, there is a strong case for targeting resources by a limited negative income tax scheme. In all these areas, reverse income tax schemes have the undoubted virtues of selectivity and (where relevant) of retaining incentives to productivity and, ultimately, independence.

As against the benefits, targeted negative income tax schemes carry significant hazards. They demand a great deal of detailed knowledge on the part of government bureaucracies, which is to say that they presuppose a large administrative apparatus capable of measuring accurately fluctuating incomes and assessing changing circumstances. Much more fundamentally, all such schemes of targeting run the risk of rewarding the imprudent. If targeting schemes are to allow for more generosity than is feasible under universal schemes, they thereby create an incentive to imprudence—most obviously in the case of targeted old age pensions. These same hazards apply to voucher schemes, targeted or universal.

The Benefits and Costs of Voucher Schemes

In regard to primary and secondary education, a voucher scheme would undoubtedly have many advantages. The present system is riddled with inequities which cry out for remedy. It is inequitable that those who elect for private schooling should in effect have to pay twice. It is inequitable that the quality of state schooling should so often depend on the neighbourhood in which a family can afford to live. It is inequitable that the poorest, whose marginal tax rates are often the highest, should also often receive the worst schooling. And it is both inequitable and socially divisive that religious communities and immigrant groups which, like the Muslim, Hindu and Jewish populations, seek a distinctive type of education for their children, should face a choice of paying for it out of taxed income or of engaging in

[52]

conflict with head teachers or local authorities or other parents over the form and content of schooling. These inequities in the existing system are obvious, and need no grand 'theory of justice' to be recognisable.

A voucher system for schools has hazards of its own, however. The introduction of a state subvention for private schooling could well weaken its independence. That this is no merely theoretical possibility is suggested by a moment's thought on what would happen if a voucher scheme were combined with current proposals for a National Curriculum. The proposed national curriculum is in any case objectionable on various grounds. It over-emphasises the vocational dimension of education at the expense of its role as an initiation into a cultural inheritance. By centralising curricular choice to an extent hitherto unheard of in England, it concentrates authority further into the hands of educational bureaucrats, who will in practice be decisive in framing and implementing it. There is, no doubt, much in the Education Reform Act that is genuinely devolutionary in passing decision-making down to the level of the school. But the proposed national curriculum embodies an indefensible degree of centralisation which would not be curbed by the introduction of a voucher system and which enhances the dangers posed to the independence of the private sector in education attendant on any voucher scheme.

The Alternative to Vouchers: Privatisation of Schooling

If we are to extricate ourselves from the present bureaucratisation of schooling, we must first of all question the very principle of a national system of schooling. In this connection we do well to recall the admonition of John Stuart Mill, uttered well over a century ago:

'A general State education is a mere contrivance for moulding people to be exactly like one another: and as the mould in which it casts them is that which pleases the predominant power in the government, whether this be a monarch, a priesthood, an aristocracy, or the majority of the existing generation; in proportion as it is efficient and successful, it establishes a despotism over the mind, leading by natural tendency to one over the body.

'An education established and controlled by the State should only exist, if it exist at all, as one among many competing experiments, carried on for the purpose of example and stimulus, to keep the others up to a certain standard of excellence. Unless, indeed, when

[53]

society in general is in so backward a state that it could not or would not provide for itself any proper institutions of education unless the government undertook the task: then, indeed, the government may, as the less of two great evils, take upon itself the business of schools and universities, as it may that of joint stock companies, when private enterprise, in a shape fitted for undertaking great works of industry, does not exist in the country.

'But in general, if the country contains a sufficient number of persons qualified to provide education under government auspices, the same persons would be able and willing to give an equally good education on the voluntary principle, under the assurance of remuneration afforded by a law rendering education compulsory, combined with State aid to those unable to defray the expense.'[1]

Mill's argument suggests that the solution to our present difficulties lies in wholesale privatisation of the schooling system. Under a low-tax régime of the sort I shall later discuss, the vast majority of families could afford to pay for their children's education themselves with the role of a voucher scheme being confined to the supplementation of very low incomes. Because of the vast savings inherent in school privatisation, the resultant tax levels would be so low that tax deductibility for school fees would also be unnecessary. Like any other form of government funding to schooling, this arrangement carries with it dangers to the independence of schools since, at the very least, government must decide what counts as a school for the purposes of funding. Mill himself, however, proposed a way in which the danger of arbitrary governmental power over schools could be obviated:

'The instrument for enforcing the law could be no other than public examinations, extending to all children and beginning at an early age. An age might be fixed at which every child must be examined, to ascertain if he (or she) is able to read. If a child proves unable, the father, unless he has some sufficient ground of excuse, might be subjected to a moderate fine, to be worked out, if necessary, by his labour, and the child might be put to school at his expense. Once in every year the examination should be renewed, with a gradually extending range of subjects, so as to make the universal acquisition, and what is more, retention, of a certain minimum of general knowledge virtually compulsory.

'Beyond that minimum there should be voluntary examinations on all subjects, at which all who come up to a certain standard of

---

[1] John Stuart Mill, *On Liberty* (1859), London: J. M. Dent, Everyman edition, 1972, p. 161.

proficiency might claim a certificate. To prevent the State from exercising, through these arrangements, an improper influence over opinion, the knowledge required for passing an examination (beyond the merely instrumental parts of knowledge, such as languages and their use) should, even in the higher classes of examinations, be confined to facts and positive science exclusively.'[1]

Streamlining the National Curriculum

In the present context, this would mean restricting the National Curriculum to the 'core' subjects of English Literature, Mathematics and Science. Such a reduced curriculum would surely be an entirely reasonable requirement for state funding. It would enable such schools as the Orthodox Jewish Yesodey Hatorah School in Stamford Hill, North London, the Islamic Zakaria Girls' School in Kirklees, Leeds, and others, to receive public funding, provided their pupils performed adequately under a restricted National Curriculum.

Here it is important to note, as a crucial part of school privatisation, that public funding need not, and should not, be restricted to vouchers for the neediest. It should also encompass (as advocated by Simon Upton, MP and others in the New Zealand National Party) a system of *Merit Bursaries* for the brightest. Such a scheme, which in the British context can be seen as an extension of the Assisted Places Scheme, embodies a sound meritocratic maxim, once institutionalised in the grammar schools—*that educational provision be related to demonstrated ability*. Such Merit Bursaries should be available to bright children from low-income families, *in addition* to whatever support is provided to them through low-cost loan schemes. Of course, private schools may opt out of both forms of government funding, if they so choose. But any school which wished to be granted this funding would have to be one which conformed to the 'core' National Curriculum.

The Millian scheme conforms to two other important maxims, which ought to commend it to us. The voucher scheme it incorporates is a targeted voucher scheme, with the bulk of the population benefiting from much lower taxes—a mix which best approximates *the direct return of purchasing power to consumers*. And it confers autonomy on families *by giving them exit rather than voice*—that is to say, it enables them, in education as elsewhere, to vote with their feet by shopping around, rather than (as

[1] John Stuart Mill, *ibid.*, pp. 161-62.

[55]

envisaged in the Education Reform Act) seeking to enhance parental power by creating a costly and burdensome apparatus of democratic participation. Wholesale privatisation of the schooling system, then, with provision for the costs of families with slender means being defrayed under a limited voucher scheme, a system of Merit Bursaries for the bright who are also needy, and probably far greater flexibility in the school-leaving age, is the best way forward for us.

Policy Towards Higher Education

Present policy towards higher education is unacceptably *dirigiste* in a variety of ways. Here I speak warily, since my own position as a university teacher opens me to charges of special pleading (and rightly so). Also, the *status quo ante* was hardly defensible, involving as it did a massive generational inequity in regard to aspiring entrants into university teaching and research. Once the unsustainable expansionism of the Sixties had come to its inevitable end, British universities were bound to enter something akin to a stationary state. In such a state, existing staff with tenure had the privileges of *rentiers*, and newly qualified academics found few or no opportunities available to them.

Nevertheless, present policies are quite manifestly misconceived. The abolition of tenure is regrettable, since it is bound to discourage mobility within the system and to lower the quality of recruitment in subjects (such as philosophy and the humanities) which lack a significant external market. Loss of tenure following upon promotion or a lateral move into another institution is a massive disincentive against mobility, which is likely to freeze the system for a generation—a curious way of promoting flexibility in it. Furthermore, a blanket government policy on tenure is inconsistent with respect for autonomous institutions and the independence of civil society. Decisions as to whether to have tenure, and on what terms, are properly taken by universities themselves, not by governments.

Action on tenure is, however, far from being the worst aspect of current policy. The real disaster is the effective nationalisation of the entire system of universities and polytechnics, with the Minister of Education arrogating to himself huge discretionary powers over hitherto autonomous institutions, and the system as a whole being subject to a *dirigiste* policy animated by the conception of universities as instruments of economic growth. This is a development replete with ironies, for it is surely absurd

[56]

that a Government which began by advocating its own withdrawal from economic life on the Hayekian ground that it inevitably lacks the information required to plan the economy should seek powers over universities so as to plan the growth of knowledge! It is yet more ironic that a commitment to civil society and autonomous institutions should be honoured by subjecting universities to the supposed requirements of economic growth. In this conception, the control of universities becomes an arm of industrial policy, and their character as institutions with their own *telos* is lost. It is obvious, further, that there is a danger to intellectual liberty in a situation in which departments can be closed at ministerial discretion. Whether ministerial judgement be based on an assessment of a subject's supposed contribution to economic growth, or on its inherent intellectual merits, it is entirely unacceptable that such decisions be within the discretionary authority of government.

What then is to be done? A return to previous arrangements is out of the question. A 'marketisation' of university education, with grants being replaced by tuition and maintenance loans and the new University Funding Council being phased out, seems a solution far better in accord with the character of universities, with the protection of liberty and, for that matter, with the present Government's earlier project of restraining the arbitrary power of the state. It is true that, for the presently foreseeable future, most university funding would remain in government hands under a loan system. The pattern and content of university teaching and research would, however, be determined by individual choice rather than ministerial fiat. A further crucial reform is the according of full tax deductibility to gifts made to universities by individuals and firms—a reform which one should have supposed to be an obvious one, given that British universities are expected by government to emulate American universities, which enjoy this privilege. It is to be hoped that some such proposal will gain support across the political spectrum, as the most feasible alternative to the present danger of a sort of mercantilism in the life of the mind.

Health Care: The Withering Away of the NHS

The objections to the NHS from the standpoint of individual liberty and consumer choice are familiar, and need little

[57]

rehearsal here.[1] In essence, they amount to the observation that the NHS is by its nature a system of rationing, with a combination of finite resources and infinite demand generating an allocation of medical care by medical and bureaucratic fiat rather than by the preferences and choices of patients. We need not claim that the NHS embodies the worst possible system of delivery of medical care, since most others—the Soviet system, with its chaos and corruption, the unreformed American system, with its ruinous inflation of medical costs, and the complicated arrangements in continental Europe—carry with them equal, similar or more serious hazards. What is clear is that no country has yet devised a set of institutions for the delivery of medical care which protects equity and liberty. The NHS is subject to particular criticism in that the allocation of resources within it is constrained by bureaucratic rigidities and, because middle-class people are better equipped with leisure time and social skills to exploit it, the allocation of resources is often regressive, disfavouring the poor and unskilled. Current proposals for the reform of the NHS, as canvassed by the present Government, are for the most part thoroughly objectionable, in that they encompass little more than the imposition of another tier of rationing on a pre-existent régime of rationing.

What is at the root of the widely perceived *malaise* of the NHS? The arguments of conventional health economists that 'health care is special' are specious, and have been effectively refuted elsewhere.[2] Such arguments presuppose what is undoubtedly everywhere, in varying degrees, a fact—a massive professional monopoly in health care, and a consequent diversion of the allocation of resources from patients to medical professionals, hospital managers and bureaucrats. My principal contention is that no policy of NHS reform can hope to succeed which does not aim, among other important objectives, to loosen the grip of professional monopoly on the supply of medical services.

A sound maxim in this area of policy is that *basic medical care should be distributed in accordance with basic medical need*. In the context of existing institutional provision, this means that any reform programme should safeguard the interests of those who

[1] For an excellent analysis, David G. Green, *Everyone a Private Patient: An Analysis of the Structural Flaws in the NHS and How They Could be Remedied*, Hobart Paperback 27, London: IEA, 1988.

[2] David G. Green, *Challenge to the NHS*, Hobart Paperback 23, London: IEA, 1986.

are uninsurable privately, such as the very old, the disabled, the chronic sick, and so on. An evolutionary reform programme would allow all who wish to opt out of NHS coverage, with insurance for those in the categories I have mentioned being underwritten by government. Within the NHS, policy should aim at the creation of *internal markets*, and at fostering the growth of such institutions as the HMO (Health Maintenance Organisation), which has been pioneered in the United States. We cannot prefigure the pattern of provision which would emerge if, in addition to these moves towards 'marketisation' within the NHS, consumers were enabled to exit from it and to recover the taxes they would otherwise have paid in its support. Most likely, a wide variety of forms of provision would spring up, especially if occupational licensure provisions were made more flexible, and professional monopoly was thereby diminished. In this scheme, the role of government would be confined to operating an NHS which would be likely to wither away, to underwriting the insurance of those who would otherwise be uninsured or underinsured, to enforcing a more liberal régime of licensure, and, in a limited exercise in paternalism, to requiring insurance from all for basic medical care, including provision against catastrophic illness.

In the context of such a reform policy, there is a strong case for an hypothecated Health Tax with an exit option. Such a tax would make visible and perceptible to consumers as taxpayers the costs of the NHS. The great majority of those who chose to exercise the option of *exit* from the hypothecated Health Tax could obtain adequate coverage without governmental subventions or further tax relief. (There is a case for hypothecated income taxation with exit options in other areas of government provision, but it is one I cannot explore here.) Those who, because of their medical history or prospects, could not do so, should receive the government subsidy mentioned earlier.

The ultimate result of this evolutionary reform package could well be a situation wherein *everyone is a private patient*,[1] where medical services are subject to individual choice and decision, rather than institutional allocation, and the basic needs of the poor and those in high-risk medical categories are fully protected. Such an outcome can be envisaged, however, only if market competition, and its precondition, a relaxation of

[1] See David G. Green's monograph, above, p. 58, footnote 1.

professional monopoly in medical care, are allowed to work their effects both within the NHS and beyond.

Pensions: The Case for Voluntary Bismarckianism

Existing national insurance systems were meant (by Beveridge) to express a sort of Bismarckian conception—the conception of a universal self-insurance as a symbol of citizenship. But existing National Insurance contributions preserve the morally dubious fiction of compulsory self-insurance, when in fact they are actuarial nonsense and amount merely to income taxation by stealth. Both employees' national insurance contributions, and employers', should in the interests of greater ethical clarity (and, in the case of employers' contributions, because they are a tax on jobs and so restrict employment opportunities) be abolished. Their full integration into income taxation, whatever the administrative difficulties of such a reform, is eminently desirable.

A voluntarist version of the Bismarckian principle is that excellent American innovation, the Individual Retirement Account (IRA), whereby money set aside for old age is tax deductible. Combined with the removal of the tax immunities of pension funds, such a reform would restore to the individual responsibility for provision for old age. As I shall later argue, however, the need for IRAs could be obviated by an even more radical move—the move to an Expenditure Tax, which exempts all savings from taxation. These are measures for the medium or longer term. In the present situation, the best we can do for old people is to maintain pensions at a reasonable level, with disregards for income for the better-off and means-tested benefits to alleviate the lot of the poorest.

Unemployment and Poverty—
Their Roots in Government Intervention

In discussing the heterogeneous range of policies and institutions that go under the head of 'the Welfare State', thus far little has been said—save by way of comments on negative income tax schemes—about the problems of poverty and unemployment. The omission of any extended discussion of these was deliberate, inasmuch as it seems clear that modern poverty, like modern unemployment, is a deep-seated problem that will not respond significantly to fine-tuning of welfare or unemployment benefits.

It is vital, first of all, to grasp that *most modern poverty*, certainly that in Britain today, *is a cultural rather than merely an economic*

[60]

phenomenon. This is to say that its origins are chiefly in family breakdown, poor education and lack of human skills rather than in sheer stringency of resources. Certainly, there are many who are old, or disabled, or chronically sick, who can and should benefit from a more generous, and better targeted, allocation of government resources. But these groups do not make up the underclass with which we should at present be most urgently concerned—that section of our society, comprising several million households, which is effectively outside the market economy, or only peripherally involved in it. Two aspects of this 'underclass' are crucially relevant to any sensible policy in regard to it.

Firstly, it is important to note that the underclass is a highly differentiated, and not at all an homogeneous category. It includes not only the long-term unemployed, but unskilled young people, impoverished pensioners, one-parent families, and diverse other groups.

Secondly, it is of the greatest moment to recognise that, for the most part, *the existing underclass is an artefact of interventionist policy.* Poverty among pensioners is, as we have already noted, a by-product of the inflation and over-taxation of earlier decades. Structural and long-term unemployment are consequences of rigidities in the economy that have been buttressed by government policies. Youth unemployment is, at least in part, a product of poor schooling, which fails to teach elementary skills of literacy and numeracy and which neglects to build up the human capital of the young. Much current poverty is tax-induced, in that the poor face higher marginal rates than any other group in society. And much unemployment is also tax-related, in that employers' national insurance payments and business rates are effectively taxes on jobs. Insofar as it boosts house prices, the current tax relief available on mortgage interest on owner-occupied dwellings also fosters unemployment by making mobility harder. Much could be done to ease unemployment and poverty if these pernicious features of our present tax régime were done away with.

Yet the hard core of structural unemployment and of cross-generational poverty is unlikely to respond to these necessary measures. What then is to be done? Far-reaching reform in education of the sort already discussed, together with measures to promote a revival of the private rented market in housing, are likely to be indispensable parts of the solution to these deep-

[61]

[handwritten at top: This whole book presumes a universally "rationally capable" population, able to maximize self-interest through informed choice]

seated problems. Training vouchers, which enable the long-term unemployed (and others) to re-skill themselves for employment, could also be of considerable value. Most centrally, perhaps, measures designed to facilitate the accumulation of capital by those who have none or little are likely to do most over the longer run to promote the gradual disappearance of the underclass.

A Pluralist Solution for Welfare?

As to the welfare state as a whole, policy ought to aim to return provision to private hands under a régime of lower taxation and targeted voucher schemes. Such voucher schemes may and ought to have a redistributional aspect, as I shall later maintain. A reform package for the welfare state should recognise also that there will always be a need for some means-tested benefits, that a voluntarist version of Bismarckian self-insurance has considerable promise, and that (partly because of the costs of targeting) there is no reason why some benefits should not be universal. (Old age pensions may be an instance of this last class, and were so recognised in the 1989 Budget.) In acknowledging that in coping with poverty and unemployment we need a mix of measures, involving unavoidable trade-offs among conflicting values, we are accepting the pluralist insight, profoundly expressed in the work of Isaiah Berlin,[1] that no single principle is adequate to morality or policy. No single measure can deal with the inheritance of earlier policy, whose consequences we now confront. The principal point that needs to be grasped by policymakers at present is that it is the institutions of the current welfare state that constitute the chief impediments to curing the ills it was set up to prevent.

Local Government and the Role of Intermediary Institutions

In a Hobbesian limited state of the sort I have been commending, what is the proper role of local government? It should be clear at once that, if the national government is to be small as well as strong, there will be much that should be done by local authorities. Recent developments in local government have in many instances been vulnerable to the legitimate criticism that they exemplify a trend towards further centralisation. At the

---

[1] For a magisterial summation of his outlook, Isaiah Berlin, 'On the Pursuit of the Ideal', *New York Review of Books*, 17 March 1988, p. 18 *et seq.*.

same time, local authorities have often performed worse in their respect for liberty than national government; they have been more invasive, less representative, more wasteful and more liable to capture by collusive interests and extremist groups. Sensible policy in this area would involve further reducing the size of local authorities, perhaps by reducing the various tiers of non-national government to a single tier of small, responsive local authorities. This would in effect be the opposite of devolution and federalism, whose advocates fail to perceive the dangers to liberty and economy in piling layer upon layer of government, with all their attendant bureaucracies. Such dangers were illustrated graphically in many of the measures introduced in this area under the Heath administration.

The question of the proper mode of funding of local government is less fundamental than the question of its size and mode of representation. It might be funded by a poll tax, as envisaged by the present Government, by a local income tax, as advocated by many of the Government's critics, or local taxation might be abolished altogether (as is virtually the case in France). Even in the last of these options, local government could still enjoy a significant margin of financial autonomy, by the operation of lotteries, by taking out loans, by the sale of their own assets which could then be reinvested for income and, most importantly, by the charging of user fees for its services. The unrepresentative character of many local authorities in recent times is likely to be diminished when, as under any of these options, there is a more direct connection between local expenditure and the costs to the local voter.

There is, in addition, a case for reconsidering the electoral system for local authorities, where plausibly a single transferable vote system would do much to restrain activist minorities, but such a proposal is beyond the scope of the present study. What is crucial is that, if local authorities were much smaller and far more numerous, they could compete far more effectively than hitherto for residents and businesses. *Promoting competition among local authorities* should be the guiding maxim for policy in this sphere.

Consideration of the place of local authorities in a limited government raises the vexed issue of the role of intermediary institutions in the kind of Hobbesian state I have advocated here. Is there a tension between the demand for a small, strong state as guardian of civil society and the independence of intermediary institutions which stand between the individual and that state? There is no necessary or inevitable tension between the two. For a strong state is a necessary condition of civil peace: government must be strong enough to defy collusive interest groups, to confront and face down over-mighty sectional interests and to uphold the rule of law. Contrary to received ideas, a state whose functions are few and which is small in size is most likely to be a strong state, capable of curbing special interests. In this sense, a strong state is a precondition of the free market and so of a flourishing civil society.

There is no incompatibility between a strong state and the intermediary institutions which are the framework of civil life. Much recent discussion has been disabled by the assumption that intermediary institutions must be governmental (or quasi-governmental) institutions. This was not so in the 19th century, when civil society in England was at its most vital. It remains a legitimate concern about developments in Britain over the past decade that (as in the case of universities) government has attempted, with some success, to make intermediary institutions its servants. This unhappy trend can be reversed, in present circumstances, only by revitalising intermediary institutions on market lines. Here one may reasonably hope, for example, that an extension of the enterprise-zone policy into inner-city areas might revive local communities and their distinctive institutions. In addition, policy should aim at fostering community by endowing distinctive cultural traditions with enabling resources on the lines I shall sketch later.

3. THE AGENDA OF DISTRIBUTION

A recent and powerful current in liberal thought has sought to contest and overthrow the assumption that government ought to have as one of its primary concerns the distribution of goods in society. In its most incisive and compelling form, this is the argument advanced by Hayek in *The Mirage of Social Justice*.[1]

Hayek's argument seems to have at least three prongs. There is first the claim that any viable market order presupposes and entails a large measure of economic inequality whose distribution is both unpredictable and uncontrollable. Secondly, there is the argument that distributive principles for important

[1] F. A. Hayek, *Law, Legislation and Liberty*, Vol. II: *The Mirage of Social Justice*, London: Routledge & Kegan Paul, 1976.

social and economic goods presuppose a value-consensus in the absence of which government intervention to implement such principles is bound to be perceived as arbitrary and coercive. Thirdly, there is the thesis that the slogan of social justice, being in itself vacuous, has in practice functioned, largely conservatively, as a legitimating formula for the protection of entrenched interest groups from the side-effects of economic change. The implicit moral of Hayek's analysis is that the concern by government with distributional issues is foolish and destructive and ought to be abandoned. On this view, government ought to confine itself to defining the rules of property and enforcing them, which together exhaust its responsibilities.

Hayek's argument against current popular and political uses of 'social justice' is devastating. It contains several decisive criticisms of current distributivist notions. There is, first, the *epistemic* insight—that the actual dispersion of incomes in the market process cannot be predicted, or even known retrospectively in its entirety, by anyone. Patterned principles of justice in distribution, even John Rawls's elegant and to many intuitively appealing Difference Principle requiring that economic inequalities be only such as are required to improve most the absolute position of the worst-off,[1] make an impossible demand on the knowledge possessed by, or available to, governments. Further, though this is a separate claim of Hayek's, the attempt to control incomes so as to match some preferred pattern of merit, need or desert, is incompatible with the effective functioning of the market, which requires that prices be undistorted so as to act as signalling devices for individuals and enterprises. *which is not ever stable*

The second point is that there is in our society not enough in the way of a consensus on basic needs which would enable us to rank them in weight when they come into practical competition with each other. And there is little doubt that the rhetoric of social justice has further enfeebled government by providing a rationale for concessions to vociferous interest groups, thereby deepening the new Hobbesian dilemma to which I have earlier alluded.

Distribution as a Concern of Policy

The idea that a limited government may safely or justifiably neglect questions of distribution is nevertheless a fatal one for

[1] John Rawls, *A Theory of Justice*, Oxford: The Clarendon Press, 1972, pp. 60-65.

[65]

policy. There is, to start with, a powerful argument in political prudence and collective self-interest for a concern with distribution. A liberal polity will not be stable, nor will its communal life be free of destructive conflict, so long as many people lack independent resources and an underclass languishes without assets or opportunities. Further, any exclusion from enjoyment of the benefits of property undermines its very *raison d'être*. Private property is justified, not only or primarily as a shield against coercion by the state, but as a condition of autonomy and independence of one's fellows. Those who lack property and are denied the opportunity to acquire it may reasonably be expected to lack the dispositions appropriate to civil life and may well become its enemies. personal property vc. private property

There is a final reason in justice for the view that all are --- entitled in a liberal civil association to an unfettered opportunity to acquire property. Existing distributions of assets are a product of historical accident rather than any defensible principle. Worse, they are plainly the result in part of manifest injustice— not least the injustice of earlier interventionist policies of confiscatory taxation and inflation. There can be no justification whatsoever for treating the existing property distribution as sacrosanct or beyond reform. Nor are present policies without a clear impact on distribution: existing tax and welfare arrangements have a bearing on the distribution of goods—income, property and human capital—that is quite evidently non-neutral. Again, radical reform of the system of transfer payments, unlike privatisation policy, is sometimes a zero-sum affair: it benefits some at the expense of others. Not for utilitarians

For all these reasons, distribution cannot avoid being on the agenda of limited government. Unless the underlying distribution of property entitlements is explicitly addressed by defenders of the market economy, they will properly be vulnerable to the socialist criticism that they are indifferent to the justice of the market order, and there will be constant demands for income redistribution. As James Buchanan has well put it:
ANARCHO - CAPITALISM
'Libertarian critics of efforts to transfer incomes and wealth should concentrate their attacks on the unwarranted use of democratic decision-structures. An open society cannot survive if its government is viewed as an instrument for arbitrary transfers among its citizens. On the other hand, libertarians go too far and reduce the scope of their argument when they reject genuinely constitutional or framework arrangements that act to promote some rough equality in

[66]

pre-market conditions and act so as to knock off the edges of post-market extremes.

'The libertarian may defend the distributive role of the competitive process on standard efficiency grounds, and he may, if he chooses, also develop ethical arguments in support of this rule. But this is not the same thing as defending the distributive results that might be observed in a market economy in which there is no attempt to adjust starting positions. The libertarian who fails to make the distinction between the two separate determinants of observed distributive results makes the same mistake as his socialist counterpart who attacks the market under essentially false pretences.'[1]

Buchanan's statement in no way legitimates egalitarianism, or sanctions the imposition on society of any preferred or desirable pattern of distribution. Robert Nozick has shown that the attempt to impose a comprehensive overall distributional pattern on society involves constant governmental intervention, continuous invasion of individual liberty, and ultimately the prohibition of capitalist acts among consenting adults.[2] From this we may derive the maxim that *respect for individual liberty entails the acceptance that there will be no overall pattern of distribution in society.*

We may go further. Hayek has argued powerfully that acceptance of a market economy involves accepting a large, and unpredictable, measure of economic inequality. In addition, historical experience suggests that attempts to 'correct' market distributions of income and capital are costly, unsuccessful and counter-productive: they generate a black or parallel economy of untaxed services, flatten out incentives (especially for risky or speculative ventures), and freeze existing inequalities. These considerations suggest a further maxim, that a successful market economy requires that *the overwhelming mass of goods and services be subject to market allocation.*

Distributional policies which conform to these maxims should seek to *supplement* market distributions rather than to 'correct' or thwart them. They should operate principally on the expenditure side, as with the Merit Bursaries and weighted vouchers and loans I have discussed—or, when they work on the taxation side, they should seek to disperse wealth rather than transfer it to the state.

[1] James Buchanan, 'Rules for a Fair Game', in *Liberty, Market and State*, Brighton: Wheatsheaf Books/Harvester Press, 1986, p. 139.

[2] R. Nozick, *Anarchy, State and Utopia, op. cit.*

'A Reasonable Spread of Endowments'

Buchanan's statement, then, in no way supports the transfer of resources from civil society to government. Instead, it affirms that the legitimacy of the free market depends on a reasonable spread in endowments. What does this mean for policy? It has, I suggest, clear implications for policy towards savings and inheritance. At present, it is virtually impossible to accumulate significant capital from income, since money invested in a bank or building society is effectively double-taxed. In order to remedy this situation, an Expenditure Tax should be instituted whereby all income that is saved or invested is tax-exempt. The administrative difficulties of such a measure are familiar and formidable, but it is the most fundamental and radical step that could be taken to allow for the accumulation of capital by those who presently have none. If such a measure were adopted, the remaining tax privileges of owner-occupation and of pension funds could reasonably be terminated. These latter are at once hard to justify in equity and serve to distort the pattern of investment. As James Meade has put the case against the present arrangements:

'A . . . mistaken policy in the housing market is the exemption of owner-occupiers from taxation on the annual value of their houses. By no means all owner-occupiers are poor. Consider rich Mr A using stock exchange dividends to rent a house from rich Mr B. Mr A will pay income tax at a high rate on his investment income and will pay rent to Mr B out of the remainder of his tax-free income. Mr B will then pay income tax at a high rate on the rent received from Mr A. This is as it should be; there are two rich men and two incomes from two important real capital assets, one from the profits of the companies whose shares are owned by Mr A, and one from the annual value of the house owned by Mr B. If now Mr A hands over his shares to Mr B and Mr B hands over the house to Mr A so that Mr A is now an owner-occupier, according to present arrangements no tax will be paid on the annual value of the house, though tax will, of course, still be payable on the investment income.

'The undesirable results of this are fourfold: first, it is a way of giving tax exemption on a most important part of the real income of owner-occupiers provided they are rich enough to pay tax, an exemption which is the more important the richer the man concerned and the higher the rate of tax to which he is liable; second, it encourages the demand for housing by the rich, since this form of investment has so important a tax privilege, and thus diverts building resources and

[68]

available land to the rich end of the market and drives up the price of houses and building land against the poorer end of the market; third, it greatly discourages the building of houses for letting as contrasted with building for owner-occupiers, although for many poorer families renting a dwelling is more feasible than purchasing a dwelling; and, fourth, by reducing in an important way the tax base, it means that the rates of taxation on the remaining sources of income must be so much the higher in order to raise total tax revenue which is needed on other budgetary grounds.'[1]

There is a case, in addition, for reform of the current pattern of inheritance taxation so as to encourage the wider dispersion of wealth. What is needed is an Accessions Tax of the sort advocated by John Stuart Mill in his *Principles of Political Economy*,[2] that is to say, a tax on the recipient, rather than on the estate. Current inheritance taxation is both inequitable and economically damaging, harming small business and thwarting a reasonable cross-generational transmission of wealth. The advantages of such an Accessions Tax have been well-stated by James Meade:

> 'Such a tax would give the maximum incentive to a wealthy citizen to dispose of his property by spreading it widely among beneficiaries who have not themselves received any substantial inheritances. At the extreme, a millionaire could avoid all duty on his estate if he split it up in many small bequests each of which went to someone who had not yet acquired any property from gifts or inheritances.'[3]

The Structure of a Liberal System of Taxation

It should be noted at this point that, whereas both Mill and Meade support a progressive Accessions Tax, they diverge on income taxation, with Meade but not Mill favouring progression there too. Here Mill is surely in the right. There is no ethical or economic case for progressivity in income taxation. It does not diminish economic inequality, and may indeed enhance it. As Hayek has noted:

> 'A . . . paradoxical and socially grave effect of progressive taxation is that, though intended to reduce inequality, it in fact helps to perpetuate existing inequalities and eliminates the most important

---

[1] James Meade, *The Intelligent Radical's Guide to Economic Policy*, London: Allen and Unwin, 1975, pp. 71-72. I do not intend to endorse Meade's proposal for taxing the annual value of houses.

[2] J. S. Mill, *Principles of Political Economy*, London, 1848, Penguin edn., 1970.

[3] James Meade, *ibid.*, p. 85.

compensation for that inequality which is inevitable in a free-enterprise society. It used to be the redeeming feature of such a system that the rich were not a closed group and that the successful man might in a comparatively short time acquire large resources. Today, however, the chances of rising into the class are probably already smaller in some countries, such as Great Britain, than they have been at any time since the beginning of the modern era. One significant effect of this is that the administration of more and more of the world's capital is coming under the control of men who, though they enjoy very large incomes and all the amenities that this secures, have never on their own account and at their personal risk controlled substantial property. Whether it is altogether a gain remains to be seen.

'It is also true that the less possible it becomes for a man to acquire a new fortune, the more must the existing fortunes appear as privileges for which there is no justification. Policy is then certain to aim at taking these fortunes out of private hands, either by the slow process of heavy taxation of inheritance or by the quicker one of outright confiscation. A system based on private property and control of the means of production presupposes that such property and control can be acquired by any successful man. If this is made impossible, even the men who otherwise would have been the most eminent capitalists of the new generation are bound to become the enemies of the established rich.'[1]

Proportional income taxation has the merit of avoiding the hazards diagnosed by Hayek. In addition, it has a clear intuitive appeal in that justice and proportionality are linked in ordinary thought and the rich man who has more to protect cannot complain if he is taxed proportionately more. The most important advantage of proportional income taxation, however, is that it separates taxation from the expenditure side of government. It indicates that, aside from inheritance taxation via an Accessions Duty, defensible redistributional measures should all be on the expenditure side.

A Progressive Accessions Tax?

It is only in regard to the Accessions Tax on inheritances that the case for progressivity is arguable. For, plainly, the incentive to spread wealth the more widely, and thereby to diminish or altogether eliminate tax liability on the part of the recipient, is stronger if, given a generous exemption, larger inheritances are

[1] Hayek, *The Constitution of Liberty*, *op. cit.*, p. 321.

[70]

taxed progressively more highly. I shall not here attempt to specify either the level of exemption, or the rate of progression, save to say that it is hard to conceive of any case for a rate on large inheritances higher than the current higher rate on income of 40 per cent. The proposal here is simply for a progressive Accessions Tax on inheritances (and analogous capital transfers) which is avoidable by the device of dispersing wealth more widely.

Abolition of Capital Gains Tax and a Flat-Rate Income Tax

The argument for an Expenditure Tax has as a natural corollary that capital gains should be tax exempt. This means that, rather than achieving a level playing field among investment media by imposing capital gains tax on owner-occupied houses, the same objective should be achieved, instead, by abolishing capital gains tax altogether. In this case, removing the tax immunities of owner-occupation would mean merely removing tax relief on mortgage interest payments.

In the liberal tax régime envisaged, there would be no taxes on capital, aside from those imposed by the Accessions Duty. These latter would be eminently avoidable and need involve no significant transfer of capital from the private sphere to government. What of income taxation? Here a bold sweep of all allowances, as reportedly suggested by Frank Field, MP, should enable massive cuts in the proportional rate to be achieved. If, in addition to the abolition of personal allowances, we incorporate the huge savings resultant from school privatisation and from the abolition of child benefits, there is further scope for reductions. If, finally, VAT were to be extended at its present rate of 15 per cent to items at present zero-rated, then it would be reasonable to aim at a flat-rate tax of 15 per cent on all income as an achievable goal, even given full integration of income taxation with the current national inheritance system. This basic rate becomes the more feasible if we take into account a separate hypothecated Health Tax with an exit option for those who wish to insure themselves privately.

Phasing Out Corporation Tax

In addition to these measures, a legitimate goal of liberal policy should be the progressive reduction, and ultimate abolition, of corporation tax. As Bracewell-Milnes has persuasively argued:

'Corporation tax is a tax either on enterprise or on business

[71]

structure or on business financing: it imposes double taxation either on corporations or on dividends or on both. As a tax on enterprise, it serves no economic purpose, since the taxable capacity of enterprise is nil. Double taxation of corporations or dividends is at variance with the liberal ideal of neutrality.'[1]

The goal of liberal policy should be the abolition of corporation tax, with revenue being derived from proportional taxes on income (with savings tax-exempt) and by a VAT on all goods and services. We may go yet further. Given continued growth in the economy, static state expenditure, and indeed the existing and prospective budget surplus, there is no reason why we should not entertain an even more radical possibility, that of a liberal tax régime in which revenue is derived overwhelmingly from taxes on expenditure, with direct taxes being in the shape only of an avoidable Accessions Tax on capital and hypothecated income taxes with exit options. Such a régime may appear impossibly remote from current circumstances, but there is nothing utopian about it. If it could be achieved, it would render the Expenditure Tax redundant, and would confine tax relief to remission of VAT on charities and other desirable causes. For the foreseeable future, however, the goal of a 15 per cent flat-rate tax on income and a corresponding 15 per cent on all goods currently VAT-taxed, including those zero-rated, seems a sufficiently radical objective.

The liberal tax régime advocated here aims to promote individual liberty, personal independence, and the diffusion of capital. It aims to even out the many distortions created by present tax policy, but without making a fetish of tax neutrality. And it incorporates an explicit concern for distributional considerations, which figure also on the expenditure side of a liberal policy.

The Redistributional Dimension of Voucher and Loan Schemes

In discussing voucher schemes, I have argued that they should be selective or targeted rather than universal, with the vast majority of people benefiting from a low-tax régime. I want now to argue that there is a case for such limited income transfer

---

[1] Barry Bracewell-Milnes, *A Liberal Tax Policy: Tax Neutrality and Freedom of Choice*, London: Libertarian Alliance (reprinted from *British Tax Review*), *Economic Notes* No. 14, 1988, p. 3.

schemes having a redistributional dimension. This is perhaps most evidently appropriate in respect of student loans, since the income of the student's family may well influence his decision on whether to go to university. For this reason, loans to students from low-income families can justifiably be made on terms that are easier than those to middle-class students. In doing this, government would honour a sound meritocratic principle and even out incentives across the various income groups. Vouchers for school education, analogously, ought to be generous for the poorest, since it is from the poverty of the human capital of the poor that their low incomes often arise.

[handwritten margin note: very small %]

Again, the limited negative income tax schemes I have advocated ought to take account of the fact that the disabled and chronically sick have often the poorest quality of life in our society and their income support should for that reason be at a higher level than for able-bodied persons. Provided cut-off rates for such redistributional measures were not in excess of 50 per cent, as with the limited negative income tax schemes argued for, there ought not to be overwhelming disincentive effects (where incentive effects are relevant at all).

In advocating such redistributional measures, we are seeking to give practical effect to Buchanan's proposition regarding the fairness of the rules governing the game of the market, and we are acknowledging the truth of Hayek's assertion that 'It is clearly possible to bring about considerable redistribution under a system of proportional taxation'.[1] Such measures can, I think, be defended for their own sake, by reference to sound principles concerning equality of opportunity. But they are also defensible by reference to the risks to the stability of the free market where attention is not given to its distributive aspects. Supporters of the free market who reject concern for distribution should be aware that they are by their indifference to the distributive background and effects of the market economy increasing the political risk that the free market will be attacked and conceivably suppressed as a result of socialist criticism of its apparent injustices.

[handwritten margin note: AS WAS EVER THE CASE → WELFAR-ISM!]

Culture as a Public Good

One area of policy often neglected by market liberals is that relating to the cultural traditions whereby a market society sustains and reproduces itself. There is a tendency to suppose that, once taxes are lowered, culture can take care of itself.

[1] F. A. Hayek, *The Constitution of Liberty*, op. cit., p. 307.

[handwritten note at bottom: HERE: The nodule of state intervention is an intellectual single-minded fetish which hides the continuing market domination]

Certainly, the present tax régime makes private support for the arts, for example, expensive and difficult, and there is a clear case for reform of taxation so that it is far easier (as in the United States) for individuals and businesses to support cultural activity. If this were done, we would be conforming to the maxim that, *where the goal is to encourage some kind of desirable development or activity which it is felt that the market underproduces, this is best achieved by tax relief rather than by direct subsidies*, which inevitably concentrate discretionary authority in quasi-governmental organisations.

It is an open question, however, whether such tax reforms are by themselves sufficient to sustain the cultural heritage on which the free market ultimately depends. Market liberals, such as Samuel Brittan and Alan Peacock, have argued persuasively that deregulation of television should be accompanied by the institution of an Arts Council of the Air with a mandate to subsidise productions the market would not of itself support.[1] Again, extending government aid (either directly, as under present arrangements, or via tax deductions or voucher schemes) to Muslim, Orthodox Jewish and Hindu schools is supported not only by considerations of equity, but also as an enabling device whereby those cultural traditions can renew and reproduce themselves. Other examples could easily be found, but my general point is more important than any specific measures. This is that *the stability of the market society depends crucially on a matrix of cultural traditions which at once legitimate it and find expression in it.* As with the National Curriculum, which fosters literacy in a common language, government may legitimately fund artistic activity so as to renew the common culture. A limited government has therefore a vital role in transmitting the values on which a market society depends. A limited government which rejects or is indifferent to the culture which underpins the market neglects one of the conditions of its own existence.

[1] Home Office, *Report of the Committee on Financing the BBC* (the Peacock Report), Cmnd. 9824, London: HMSO, 1986; and discussion of the proposal in both Alan Peacock's and Samuel Brittan's chapters in Cento Veljanovski (ed.), *Freedom in Broadcasting*, Hobart Paperback 29, London: Institute of Economic Affairs, 1989.

[74]

IV. CONCLUSION:
MARKET LIBERALISM AND THE FUTURE

'Canst thou draw out leviathan with a hook? or his tongue with a
cord which thou lettest down? Canst thou put a hook into his
nose? or bore his jaw through with a thorn? Will he make many
supplications unto thee? Will he speak soft words unto thee? Will
he make a covenant with thee? Will thou take him for a servant
forever?'   *Job*, 41: 1-4.

'Free relations among free men—this precept of ordered anarchy
can emerge as a principle when a successfully renegotiated social
contract puts 'mine and thine' in a newly defined structural
arrangement and when the Leviathan that threatens is placed
within new limits.'

JAMES BUCHANAN[1]

[handwritten margin note: when was it ever more than a hypothesis]

The argument for limited government is one that is addressed
across the political spectrum. Market liberalism is a perspective
that should be compelling both for conservatives, who affirm the
foundation of market institutions in an historical inheritance of
norms and traditions, and for social democrats, who seek to
reform that inheritance by reference to general principles of
equality. By market liberalism I mean the proposition that the
great bulk of economic activity is best conducted within the
institutions of market capitalism in a régime of private property
and contractual liberty. And by limited government I mean a
form of government which restricts itself to setting the framework of market capitalism (a framework that encompasses, I
have argued, policy which addresses the distributional and
cultural pre-conditions of a stable market order).

The political debate between free-market conservatism and a
market-oriented social democracy is one that should focus on
such issues as distribution, the scope and variety of public goods,
and the best policy for supporting intermediary institutions and
flourishing communal life. For this debate to occur and be
fruitful, however, it is vital that market liberalism be accepted

[1] James Buchanan, *The Limits of Liberty: between Anarchy and Leviathan*, Chicago: University
of Chicago Press, 1975, p. 180.

[75]

too bloody right!

across the political spectrum as the only set of institutions which can in a modern society protect values of liberty, independence, equity and prosperity. This in turn presupposes that delusive visions such as market socialism be taken off the intellectual agenda. Social democrats should be encouraged in this move by the experience of the communist states, where there is growing recognition that 'market socialism' describes nothing that is defensible or achievable. They should listen to J. Kornai, one of the intellectual leaders of the Hungarian economic reform movement, when he says of the theorist of market socialism, Oskar Lange:

as evidence? of what?

Are they not a select portion of society always?

> 'Lange's model is based on erroneous assumptions regarding the "planners". The people at his Central Planning Board are reincarnations of Plato's philosophers, embodiments of unity, unselfishness and wisdom. They are satisfied with doing nothing else but strictly enforcing the "Rule" ... Such an unworldly bureaucracy never existed in the past and will never exist in the future. Political bureaucracies have inner conflicts reflecting the divisions of society and the diverse pressures of various social groups. They pursue their own individual and group interests, including the interests of the specialised agency to which they belong. Power creates an irresistible temptation to make use of it. A bureaucrat must be interventionist because that is his role in society; it is dictated by his situation. What is not happening in Hungary with respect to detailed micro-regulation is not an accident. It is rather the predictable, self-evident result of the mere existence of a huge and powerful bureaucracy. An inherent tendency to recentralisation prevails.'[1]

It is important to note that Kornai's incisive critique applies not only to the centralised market socialism advocated by Lange, in which government uses various devices to simulate market prices, but also to the market socialism of competing worker co-operatives that is currently fashionable in the West. This latter market socialism is unstable and unworkable for reasons closely analogous to those which condemn the Lange model as unfeasible. As the Yugoslav example has shown, self-managed worker co-operatives are risk-averse; tending slowly to consume capital rather than to invest in technological innovation, they produce structural unemployment because of their resistance to new entrants, and they cannot avoid involvement in a political competition for capital from the state investment banks. Where

[1] J. Kornai, 'The Hungarian Reform Process', *Journal of Economic Literature*, Vol. XXIV, No. 4, December 1986, pp. 1,687-1,737. The quotation cited comes from pp. 1,726-27.

it is not a recipe for economic stagnation, market socialism is a mirage, an attempt to reap the benefits of market pricing without allowing for the market pricing of the most important productive factor, capital itself, and without permitting the necessary condition of free markets, which is a system of private property in which incentives and risks are decentralised in a régime of liberal ownership.

Western social democrats must recognise that, as well as incurring substantial costs in terms of economies of scale, under-investment and structural unemployment, market socialism is inherently unstable. Both experience and theory suggest that it is bound to mutate in the potentially politically explosive direction of reinventing the central institutions of market capitalism, or else return by the route of recentralisation to a socialist command economy. It would be a hopeful augury for Britain if, in future, debate were to focus on the cultural and moral preconditions of market liberalism, rather than on the question *not the* of whether market capitalism is to be accepted—a question *same* which historical experience has in any case already decisively *in all* answered. Public discourse is now best addressed to the issue of *places.* the appropriate standards and measures for reform of market *Very* capitalism—not to delusive (or disastrous) alternatives to it. *simplistic* Indeed, the long-term survival of the free market in Britain depends ultimately on such an intellectual realignment within the major political parties, in which acceptance of market liberalism is at the heart of a new public consensus.[1]

The argument for limited government and for the market economy is not in the end an economic argument. It is an ethical argument—the argument that, in the conditions of a modern society, only market institutions can give practical realisation to the values of liberty and human dignity. The argument for the market is not the argument that government be conceived of as an economic enterprise, but rather the contrary. It is the argument that only market institutions allow free individuals to opt into, or out of, enterprise. At present, when government speaks to us in the harsh accents of Bentham rather than the civilised tones of Hume, we face the danger of civil society being further weakened by the metamorphosis of the state itself into an enterprise association. It has been the argument of this *Hobart*

[1] In this connection, the recent formation of the Radical Society, a meeting point for free-market conservatives and market-oriented social democrats, may prove to be a hopeful augury.

Paper that only the reassertion of the project of a limited government with positive tasks can hope to protect us from the spectacle, tragic or farcical as it may turn out to be, of a *dirigiste* Behemoth, in whose wake nothing is left but a litter of ephemeral corporatist projects and the ruins of civil society.

QUESTIONS FOR DISCUSSION

1. What is 'the new Hobbesian dilemma'?

2. Why is government bound to fail in its attempts to impose a preferred pattern on market distribution of income and wealth?

3. What are the main costs and hazards of a universal negative income tax?

4. Why are legal and constitutional provisions, taken by themselves, insufficient to protect economic liberties? Answer with reference to examples.

5. 'Monetarist policies presuppose a measure of control of the money supply that is incompatible with extensive financial deregulation'. Discuss.

6. 'The existing "underclass" is to a considerable degree the product of earlier interventionist policies by government'. Explain and assess this claim.

7. What are the risks of 'targeting' social benefits?

8. Why is inflation inequitable?

9. How and why do the institutions of the present British welfare state redistribute resources regressively?

10. Why must the NHS restrict consumer choice of medical care?

READINGS FOR FURTHER STUDY

Berlin, I. (1969): *Four Essays on Liberty*, Oxford: Oxford University Press.

Brittan, Samuel (1988): *A Restatement of Economic Liberalism*, London: Macmillan.

Buchanan, J. M. (1975): *Limits of Liberty: Between Anarchy and Leviathan*, Chicago: University of Chicago Press.

—— (1986): *Liberty, Market and State: Political Economy in the 1980s*, Brighton: Harvester/Wheatsheaf.

Buchanan, J. M., R. E. Wagner, J Burton (1978): *The Consequences of Mr Keynes*, Hobart Paper 78, London: Institute of Economic Affairs.

Buchanan, J. M., and H. Geoffrey Brennan (1981): *Monopoly in Money and Inflation: The Case for a Constitution to Discipline Government*, Hobart Paper 88, London: IEA.

Gray, John (1983): *Mill on Liberty: A Defence*, London: Routledge.

—— (1986): *Hayek on Liberty*, 2nd edition, Oxford: Basil Blackwell.

—— (1986): *Liberalism*, Milton Keynes: Open University Press.

—— (1989): *Liberalisms: Essays in Political Philosophy*, London: Routledge.

Hayek, F. A. (1960): *The Constitution of Liberty*, London: Routledge and Kegan Paul.

—— (1978): *Denationalisation of Money: The Argument Refined*, Hobart Paper 'Special' (No. 70), 2nd edition, London: Institute of Economic Affairs.

—— (1982): *Law, Legislation and Liberty*, one-volume edition, London: Routledge.

—— (1988): *The Fatal Conceit: The Errors of Socialism*, Collected works of F. A. Hayek, Vol. 1, London: Routledge.

Meade, James (1975): *The Intelligent Radical's Guide to Economic Policy*, London: George Allen and Unwin.

Mill, J. S. (1848): *Principles of Political Economy*, Penguin Edn., Harmondsworth: Penguin Books, 1970.

Oakeshott, Michael (1962): *Rationalism in Politics*, London: Methuen.

—— (1975): *Hobbes on Civil Association*, Oxford: Basil Blackwell.

—— (1989): *The Voice of Liberal Learning*, edited by T. Fuller, New Haven: Yale University Press.

Simon, Henry C. (1948): *Economic Policy for a Free Society*, Chicago: University of Chicago Press.

Some IEA Papers on
Government and the Economics of Politics

Readings 18
The Economics of Politics
JAMES M. BUCHANAN, CHARLES K. ROWLEY, ALBERT BRETON,
JACK WISEMAN, BRUNO FREY, A. T. PEACOCK,
and seven other contributors. Introduced by JO GRIMOND
1978   £3·00

'. . . bureaucrats are seen as trying to increase the size of their staff
and the responsibilities of their departments, in much the same way
as a small businessman strives to increase his profits.

'Politicians . . . have other goals. They are basically bidding for
votes . . . They will also . . . try to outbid each other with promises
of good things to the electorate. This—the theory argues—is an
inevitable consequence of the way democracies take decisions.'
Frances Cairncross, *Guardian*

Hobart Paper 78
The Consequences of Mr Keynes
J. M. BUCHANAN, JOHN BURTON, R. E. WAGNER
1978   £1·50

'The case for exorcism is put in the latest Hobart Paper. Three
economists, two American and one British, analyse the misuse of
economic theory for political profiteering and put proposals for
constitutional disciplines. The first and foremost proposal is that the
budgets must balance.'   Charles Pritchard, *Yorkshire Post*

'In order to provide against irresponsible budget deficit financing,
the authors of the booklet call for a written rule for the British
Parliament that there should be no budget deficit.'
Leader in *Yorkshire Post*

'. . . a thoughtful, well-written and substantive Paper.'
Accountancy

Hobart Paper 109
Government As It Is
*The impact of public choice economics on the judgement of
collective decision-making by government and on the teaching
of political science*
WILLIAM C. MITCHELL
with a Commentary by DAVID G. GREEN
1988   £4·00

'. . . the Institute of Economic Affairs is probably the most valuable voluntary body in the land. It has just produced a pamphlet, "Government As It Is", by an American, Professor William C. Mitchell, with a British Commentary by David Green. Every public figure in Britain ought to read it.'   Brian Walden, *The Sunday Times*

Hobart Paper 111
The Invisible Hand in Economics and Politics
A Study of the Two Conflicting Explanations of Society:
End-States and Processes
NORMAN P. BARRY
1988   £6.50

Occasional Paper 77
Beyond the Welfare State
An economic, political and moral critique of indiscriminate
state welfare, and a review of alternatives to dependency
RALPH HARRIS
1988   £2.00
'Ralph Harris . . . re-emphasises the timeless truths and uncanny prescience of the classical English and Scottish liberal economists . . . [offering] an instructive critique of fashionable heresy that should provoke misgiving and repentance in the estates of the realm.'
                                      Arthur Seldon (*Preface*)

Hobart Paper 90
Monopoly in Money and Inflation: The Case for
a Constitution to Discipline Government
H. GEOFFREY BRENNAN and JAMES M. BUCHANAN
1981   £1.50
'. . . trenchantly argued . . . Distrusting government—and advisers as well no doubt—Professors Brennan and Buchanan conclude that enforceable constitutional rules governing money creation are necessary if inflation is to be controlled. They make a strong theoretical case.'   Professor Geoffrey Maynard, *The Banker*

Hobart Paper 70
Denationalisation of Money
–*The Argument Refined*
F. A. HAYEK
1976   2nd edition 1978   £2·00
'The book is of interest not only because of [his] radical proposal and the arguments that support it, but also because it is a statement of the latest views on monetary policy by a Nobel Laureate whose earlier work in monetary economics was cited as one of the reasons for receiving the prize.'   David H. Howard,
                                      Journal of Monetary Economics